182
BEST PLACES
TO
MEET MEN

Get The Guy You Want

About the Author

Like many women these days, Ana Wilde is a full-time juggler of multiple roles. She is a writer, researcher and publisher, owner of a small business, and the creator of a website or six including her main blog LoveFromAna.com. She lives with her husband and two kids in an old house in Scotland, where she is chief cook and bottle washer as well as finder of all lost things.

182
BEST PLACES
TO
MEET MEN

Ana Wilde

Love From Ana.com

First Printing: 2014
Printed in the United States of America

Cover image: depositphotos.com pablonis

Contents

HOW TO
MEET MEN

There are around three and a half billion men on the planet and every big city has hundreds of thousands, sometimes millions, of men. How come it feels like there are no great men out there or that all the best ones are taken?

Are all the eligible local single guys in hiding? Are they cooped up in their living rooms, watching TV?

Well, I expect a good proportion of them are (either that, or playing video games). But they have to go out sometimes.

And great guys really are out there, getting on with their lives. They're not always in the places you go with your friends on a Saturday night, looking for "the one," but they are out there somewhere, and in more places than you could shake a stick at.

This book will show you a whole host of places where eligible guys hang out. You'll see how many options you have for meeting guys and how much fun you can have while you do.

That in itself will be an eye-opener, especially if you confine yourself to a few local haunts and activities at the moment.

But knowing those places and having those options won't do you any good by itself. You have to get yourself out there and get to know those guys, so the book will cover how you do that too.

Wishing Doesn't Work

To get a great guy, you have to go to the right places and do the right things. It's no good just wishing.

It's like landing a dream job. You're not going to get a great job by hoping one lands in your lap. Dream jobs are out there, but everyone is after them. You have to know what you want, find a suitable vacancy and then present yourself in the best possible light.

It's no different with a dream guy.

You won't land every job you go after. You won't land every guy either.

But one thing you know for a fact is that you'll have more chance of getting what you want if you have a plan and follow it.

To get a job you have to dust off your qualifications and resume, turn up at interviews looking your best and show the recruiter what an asset you could be to the company.

It's not much different when you're looking to get a guy. You need to make sure sure you're ready to impress, go where he hangs out and show him how you could be the best thing that ever happened to him.

Luckily you have the solution in your hands right now - your blueprint for meeting guys.

There's no need to ever let the words "I never meet anyone worth dating" cross your lips again.

What You'll Discover In This Book

The main idea behind this book is not just to provide a list of places for meeting guys, although you'll find plenty of ideas here. It's a whole plan for finding and attracting a guy who is right for you. There's so much more to this than being seen out and about on a Saturday night decked out in your best finery and flirting with anyone who catches your eye.

In this book, you'll discover

- How to make sure you succeed in finding Mr. Right (and what you might be doing that is stopping you)

- How to work out who exactly is right for you (and who you don't want to meet)
- The best places to discover guys that are right for you
- What to do, once you find a hot guy, to get that first important date with him.

WHERE YOU'RE GOING WRONG

There are lots of single women out there bemoaning the fact that there are no decent available guys. Yet, every day women in your city are going out on first dates, becoming part of a couple and getting married. So where are you going wrong?

Don't worry, there's really nothing wrong with you. It's not because you're not a stick-thin supermodel. Neither are all those women who are getting engaged and married. But there are a few things you might need to change...

You Hang Out With Too Many Girls

Hanging out with a big crowd of girls is never going to help you land a man. Unless a man is very confident (and then he is most likely a player and no good for a long term boyfriend), he is going to be intimidated by your friends, and is unlikely to single you out, even if you are the best of the bunch.

He might look your way, but he probably won't approach you.

Choose just one or two friends to go out with (and no more) and don't act like you're joined at the hip.

You Do Girlie Things

Whenever I go out with my girlfriends, we like to go to a nice restaurant or upmarket wine bar. Sometimes we go and see a romantic comedy. We might go shopping and have lunch. Or have a spa day.

Who do we see whenever we go to these places? Groups of women! Couples, in some places - and it's usually obvious the guy has been dragged along, and feels like a fish out of water.

Now socializing with female friends is great. There's nothing wrong with that at all, but if your whole social life consists of doing those things girls love to do, you are missing a lot of opportunities to meet guys.

If your budget and/or time for nights out is limited, suggest going to places where men hang out, at least some of the time. There are lots of suggestions coming up for great places to hang out where guys outnumber women so investigate some of these.

You Seem Desperate

If you spend your whole time looking for a man when you're out and about, that is going to be pretty obvious to everyone around you. It is pretty annoying for your friends too. But even if they are not insulted (they might be doing this too), it is pretty off-putting to guys to see a woman who obviously has nothing more on her mind than looking for a man.

Go out to have a good time and make sure you enjoy yourself whether you meet a man or not! This is easier if you go to places where the focus is on some activity other than chatting, drinking and dancing.

You may be keen to get a boyfriend but there's no reason not to have a good time while you find him. Desperation smacks of not thinking very highly of yourself. And, guess what! If you don't think much of yourself, neither will he.

You Hide Away At Home

If you are a bit of a homebody and don't go out much, then you are drastically cutting down your chances of meeting anyone at all, never mind your dream guy. He is unlikely to knock on your door, that's for sure, unless you're secretly in love with the pizza delivery guy.

Remember, there is a guy who is right for you within 50 miles of your house at all times. Where he isn't, is in your house, unless you've already met him (and then what are you doing reading this book)?

If you don't know anyone to go out with, start to expand your social circles. A lot of the things I am going to suggest in later chapters can be done alone, and you will meet potential friends as well as guys. Don't just focus on men if your social life sucks. Everyone needs a great pool of female buddies too.

You Don't Have A Plan

If you don't know what you want or how to achieve it, you're unlikely to succeed. You may have the "hoping for the best" plan or "a someday my prince will come" plan.

How has that worked for you so far?

I thought so!

Follow the plan in the next section of this book and get REAL results.

You Haven't Prioritized Your Quest

Meeting a man is going to take some time and effort, but, hey, when did anything worth having ever come without taking any kind of action?

If you want to get a boyfriend, you have to do what it takes. That includes looking your best, spending time knowing what you want, being generally sociable and actually going on dates! If your whole life is taken up with work or family or other obligations, you're not giving yourself a chance. Even if you find a great guy, you have no room for him in your life, so there's no point!

But no one is too busy to find love. If you think you don't have time, you're kidding yourself. If high powered political figures and captains of industry can manage to hold a relationship, you can certainly find time for that side of your life. You just have to switch your priorities if you don't want to stay single.

In fact, imagine Mr. Right came along tomorrow and asked you out. Would you say, "Sorry, I'm too busy at work, I've got to fit in the gym and my house is a mess I need to sort out it." You wouldn't, would you? You'd fit him in somehow. And when you fall in love with that guy, you won't be saying, "Sorry, no time for a night on the sofa watching a movie with you, I have catch up with my bills." Instead you'd be giving him top priority.

So why would you not spend time and effort finding him, when you're happy to spend time and effort once you've got him? It makes no sense. It's like saying I'll spend time writing my resume once I've got the job.

You Won't Accept A Date From Anyone But Mr. Right

Don't expect love at first sight and angels singing the moment you set eyes on a guy. It's a wonderful thing when that happens.

But this isn't the movies. This is real life.

Dating is a kind of sifting activity. You can't evaluate whether a guy is right for you without getting know him a bit, unless you actively dislike him when you meet him.

If he seems like a good guy, and there's even the faintest spark of attraction, give him a chance, and he may grow on you. People do.

Look at all those work colleagues who eventually get together after months (sometimes years) of not considering each other romantically. Respect, love and attraction grow when you give someone time.

And don't worry, going on a date with someone who doesn't immediately make your heart race is not settling for second best. That's only true if you date and then find out he's not quite right for you and still go out with him. That's settling. Until you know him, you can't decide whether it's settling or not.

You have to date to find the right man, not find the right man and then date him.

You Are Impatient Or Lack Belief

Finding the right guy takes time. If you're impatient you might throw in the towel too soon and resign yourself to a single life, deciding it's not worth the effort to even try to meet someone new.

You have to believe that the right guy is out there (in fact, there will always be many guys – perhaps many thousands – who would be right for you, not just one).

Don't give up after meeting a handful of guys online and finding none of them are right, or trying a couple of places in this guide and not meeting anyone.

Don't say, "Oh I tried that once and it didn't work." Just keep on trying new things, meeting new people and you'll succeed. You can have a lot of fun exploring your options, so you have nothing to lose.

You Distrust Men

Keep a positive mindset about guys, in general. If you dislike and distrust men and think the world is full of creeps and players, it comes across in your attitude to all men. You're right, some guys are positively Neanderthal and not fit for dating or a relationship, but there are millions of wonderful guys in the world too. Don't forget about them.

10

You Keep The Best You For Nights Out

You never know when Mr. Right is going to show up, so don't slob around in old clothes and unwashed hair wherever you go, whether it's just to the grocery store or walking the dog.

Similarly, don't reserve your kindness or cheerfulness for special occasions either. Being upbeat, polite and positive will make you and everyone else feel better. And you never know who's watching or who the people you meet could introduce you to.

If you're generally friendly and open, then you'll come across as the kind of woman many guys would like to go out with, so make sure you're that kind of woman wherever Mr. Right could be. And that's just about anywhere.

HOW TO SUCCEED
IN FINDING LOVE

There are just three steps to success in any goal and it's no different for finding a man. Of course, the devil is in the details but we'll get to all that!

1. Know What You Want

It seems somehow desperate to know exactly what you want (a life partner) and go all out to get one. But you don't have to act desperate to find a guy who's right for you. You just have to be proactive.

Mr. Right is unlikely to knock at your door any time soon. It's going to take a bit of effort to find him. Until you acknowledge what you want for your life, you may not make yourself do what it takes, especially if some of the things you need to do put you a little outside your comfort zone.

The trouble with staying within your comfort zone is that it will keep you exactly where you are – without a guy – so you have to stretch yourself a bit. And you only do that by knowing what you want and being determined to get it.

And, of course not every guy will be Mr. Right. We'll look at exactly the kind of guy you'd like to meet in a later section.

2. Put A Plan Together

You may feel determined to find a partner in your head. But that desire and determination need to translate into action if you're going to succeed. What action should you be taking? That's where a plan comes in.

Once you know what you want, we are going to systematically go through the whole process of how to get exactly that by tailoring a plan, one that will suit your circumstances, likes and dislikes as well as the outcome you want.

3. Follow The Plan

Once you have your plan, your only job is to follow it!

Don't worry, we'll look at ways of making it as easy as possible to stick to your plan and you will get there by moving forward, one step at a time. Even tiny steps will do it.

If you ever start thinking, "Is it really worth making an effort to do this?" "I'm OK by myself," or "I don't really need a man," it's probably just because you're trying new things and expanding your comfort zone a bit. But remember, your comfort zone is what keeps you stuck right where you are.

If you start doubting, remind yourself why you're doing this. To help, take a look at Appendix A, "Is Finding A Boyfriend Worth The Effort?" but don't read it unless you're chickening out of following your plan. (I don't want to depress you with the disadvantages of being single before you actually get going, because you are going to find a guy IF you follow your plan.)

Your Plan

Before putting together your own personal guy-getting having-more-fun plan, you need to get an idea of the whole process.

Although you'll find the section on putting your personal plan together towards the end of the book, it's never too soon to start thinking about some of the things it might include.

As you go through the book, make a note of anything you think you need to do to make yourself ready to meet Mr. Right, any ideas about who you'd like to meet and anything that interests you in terms of places and ways to meet men. These notes will be useful later.

WHO DO YOU WANT TO MEET?

Thinking about the kind of guy you want to meet is an essential part of your plan.

You may already know!

Lots of women have a kind of shopping list in their heads (or even on paper) about who they want to meet – their ideal guy. They have the idea if they go into as much detail as they can, picturing the guy and making him seem as close to reality as possible, he will somehow show up in their lives exactly like that.

But how many people do you know who that has worked for? I don't know any!

Having too many detailed requirements is not helpful when it comes to putting you in the right frame of mind to meet Mr. Right. Chances are with that kind of shopping list, you will walk right past the guy that could be a passionate, lifelong and perfect partner for you. You just won't recognize him!

You see, there's no such thing as a single Mr. Right. There are lots of guys who would be right for you, thousands, in fact. By picturing one guy, who does not even exist except in your imagination, you are severely limiting your choices, perhaps closing off every opportunity you'll have to meet a great guy.

Your chances of meeting that one guy are close to nil. Has it ever happened like that for anyone? No doubt it has at some point in history. Is it likely to happen that way for you? I wouldn't bet my future on it if I were you.

In fact, you need to get the whole idea of perfection out of your head, when it comes to guys. Guys are human beings, not robots. If you're looking for a robot, you'll be a long time waiting. When Mr. Right comes along, you can sure that there will be something you won't like about him, hopefully a minor detail (or six). If he's

Mr. Right, his "flaws"will be things you can live with, even love him for.

Remember you are also human and not perfect. If you find the perfect guy, how will you ever live up to his standard? You might spend your life worrying that he will leave you, because you don't quite match up to him.

Should You Settle For Mr. Wrong?

Having said that you should not look for perfection, I don't mean that you should settle for a guy who is not worthy of you, or who could not make you happy.

There are certain things that should be deal breakers for any relationship. And there are certain things you personally need in yours.

This is where having a sensible list comes in.

You need to think about what you need and set boundaries which cannot be crossed. Here's a general list that I think most of us should be looking for in a happy, well-balanced relationship. For the best chance of things working out and growing old with your guy, you want someone who is:

- kind to you and others
- trustworthy
- honest and faithful
- optimistic and generally happy and upbeat

Some things that are less important, but which may be important to you are that he is

- Confident/happy in his own skin
- Ambitious and going places
- Family oriented (loves his parents/siblings)

17

- Not anti-kids (if you want children in the future) even if he's not into them yet

And there are the negative qualities you absolutely don't want in your life. You don't want a guy who has problems with anger or jealousy, the addict, the layabout, the one who borrows money from you and never pays it back, because that way lies a lot of pain and anguish ahead.

After that, think about your interests and values, as well as the type of personality you tend to gel with.

As far as interests go, don't expect Mr. Right to share everything you do, or that you will share every interest he has. It will be utterly boring if you spend every minute of your free time together. But you do want to have some things in common so that you're happy to spend large chunks of time with him.

To this end, it's good to look for a broadly compatible type of guy. For example, if you spend every weekend hiking then it would be good to find a guy who likes the great outdoors, so you can actually see each other. If you're into the arts, look for a cultured, well-educated guy. He might not share your exact passion for Impressionist paintings or avant-garde movies but at least he'll probably understand what you see in these things and be willing to give them a try without grumbling too much.

As for values, think about what is truly important to you. If you're big on health, you will probably want to avoid the guy who drinks heavily or smokes and never gets any exercise. If you love parties, the introvert who likes to stay home all the time is probably not your Mr. Right.

You'll notice we haven't mentioned looks here. It IS important that you find your guy attractive. There has to be some kind of spark there that sets things off. But there are so many elements to

18

attraction that it's almost impossible to prescribe how Mr. Right will look.

Attraction is made up not only of looks, but also how he expresses himself, his body language, how he moves and how he interacts with you, so this should be the area where you are the most flexible. You might think you want someone tall, dark and handsome but then you fall head over heels for a blond who is just a bit taller than you, and who you find attractive because of his cheeky smile and ability to make you laugh.

The thing is, if you have tall, dark and handsome fixed in your head as a deal-breaker, you will miss out on the cheeky blond who is just right for you.

General Type

You can meet guys anywhere, so it's not essential to have a general type in mind, but if you do, you can target those places where he is most likely to show up. For example, if you love sporty guys you're more likely to bump into them at the stadium or gym than at the art gallery.

In the section of the book on the many places to meet your Mr. Right, you'll see that each option has an explanation for the type of guys you're most likely to find there, and that will help you narrow down your options.

Think about whether you like guys who are

- Sporty
- Cultured
- Party Animals
- Professional
- Altruistic
- Wealthy
- Animal lovers

19

- Geeky or Academic
- Fashion Conscious

or any other type you know you like. That's not to say that a guy couldn't be more than one type or that you are limited to only one. You may have a professional guy who is sporty on weekends, or an altruistic type who gives his time freely to charity but also loves parties. You can then meet your professional, sporty guy or your party-loving altruist in two kinds of venues.

BE PREPARED

When you're preparing to meet the guy of your dreams, it's about so much more than getting yourself looking good for a night out.

Sure, it does help if you look your best but you also have to be ready to do what it takes to get your guy and you need to be in the right mindset for a relationship, if that's what you want.

With that in mind, let's look at how best to be prepared for your guy-getting mission.

Be The Woman Of HIS Dreams

You've thought about what you want, so now is the time to think about what he is probably looking for. And it's not always a sex-mad supermodel! Guys care about looks and sexiness, of course they do, but when you talk to them about what they are really looking for, they want mostly the same qualities you do, but with a feminine touch.

So the best thing to think about is whether you match up to your own list of what you want to see in a guy.

If you want someone who is kind, be kindness personified, as your kind guy is unlikely to go after someone mean-spirited. If you want someone honest and who has integrity, be sure to have those qualities yourself to make sure that your Mr. Right respects you. If you want someone slim and healthy, how slim and healthy are you?

Do everything you can to be the best version of you, the one who can match up to the values you care about in him.

Be Ready To Be Feminine

So many of us are used to doing everything for ourselves. We have a career, we have a life, we have a home and we manage everything just fine without a guy. It's good to be independent. In fact, it's much more attractive than coming across as a needy woman.

However, there's another side to this coin, where you are so determined to be independent it can come across as having no place for him in your life.

It's a fine balance that you have to draw between being needy and allowing him to feel you want him as a man. But the upshot is that you shouldn't be afraid to ask him for advice or help. That promotes the feeling that he is able to offer something, to be your protector even in small ways. Be gracious if he opens doors for you, offers you his seat or his coat.

Be Confident

Confidence is one of the most attractive traits in a new partner and it is also one of those qualities you need to be able to interact with guys you come across as you look for Mr. Right. So if you are shy or have problems with self-esteem, it's important to work on these so that you have more chance of catching the eye of a guy and getting to know him.

Confidence is all in your head. There's a stream of positive or negative thoughts about yourself running through your mind. You feel you can't control them, but thinking negative thoughts about yourself is simply a bad habit you have to break. Every time you catch yourself with a negative thought, stop it and replace it with a positive one. It will take some effort but eventually you will feel much better about yourself.

Have a Life Of Your Own

If you are one of those women simply waiting around for your real life to begin once Mr. Right shows up, I have news for you. He isn't ever going to appear if you just sit around waiting for him. Or if he does show up, he's not going to find what you have to offer very attractive even if you are supermodel material.

When a guy goes out with you, unless he is a player just looking for sex, he is assessing much more than your looks. He is thinking about what his life would be like if you were his girlfriend. If you bring nothing to the table but your own needy self then that's not a great proposition for him. But if you have a life of your own, with a social life, friends, interests, likes and dislikes that he can relate to, then you enrich his life so much more. He can see himself fitting into and enjoying your lifestyle and enjoying his time with you.

There is even more benefit to developing yourself in this way. You'll have a lot more fun while you're single, you'll meet more guys and you'll have somewhere to suggest for those initial awkward dates other than a straightforward, run-of-the-mill dinner date.

Practice Talking To Strangers

When you meet Mr. Right, chances are he is going to be a stranger, so if you never talk to anyone outside your circle of family and friends, you need to get some practice talking to those you don't know.

Many women clam up when it comes to talking to a guy they are attracted to and the way to circumvent that awkwardness is to get comfortable talking to strangers and to treat him as any other stranger.

After all, until you get to know him he's just another stranger that you like the looks of. He might be a total dead loss once he opens his mouth and not worthy of your attention, so don't treat him any differently until he earns it.

There's no need to start a long and weighty conversation. A simple "Hi!" and one quick sentence is enough to establish contact, but the more you do this every day, with every kind of stranger, young and old, male and female, the better you will get at it.

Looking Good

Although looks are not everything, they do count in the initial stages of getting him to notice you and spark his interest, so put your best foot forward here.

Make sure you're clean, well-groomed and wearing appropriate clothes and makeup all the time, not just when you think you might meet a guy. Guys are everywhere, so imagine whenever you go out you'll be bumping into Mr. Right a few blocks down the road. Do you look the way you would want to be seen by him? If not, do something about it.

Sort out your wardrobe, make sure your hair looks right (get a great cut and color if necessary) and practice wearing just enough makeup and not too much. The right amount of makeup is where you look better than you do without it, but he doesn't worry about your face coming off on his shirt or about what you really look like under your "mask."

When it comes to clothes, wear something that suits you and shows off your figure and personality. This doesn't mean letting it all hang out with cleavage and legs everywhere, so he looks at your body and not your face. Your clothes can skim your body so he can see your shape. They don't need to be skin tight.

If you're hoping to attract a guy, remember that the fashion world doesn't do you any favors in that regard most of the time. The latest looks might impress your friends but they won't turn his head unless it's to stare and wonder what possessed you to choose that outfit. Most high fashion is going to look ridiculous to him unless you are stick thin, and actually are a supermodel.

If you are fashion conscious, pick the looks on the right side of weird and those that keep you looking like a woman. You have to be a very feminine woman to be able to look stunning to a guy when you're wearing a tux or workmen style trousers.

Set Aside Time And Money For Your Efforts

If you're going to meet guys then you have to go out. Men are not going to be forming a line outside your door. And going out takes time and money. It takes time to get ready and look good and you may need money to spend on clothes, beauty treatments and makeup to look your best. You can minimize your spending if you don't have much money, but it won't be free of charge. So set aside a budget and think about how you are going to fit in the time you need to find a guy into your busy schedule.

If you are ultra busy, you can just start your guy finding mission with your normal activities as long as you are out and about and not hiding away in your office the whole time. But remember, you'll need time for dates and ultimately you'll need to spend a lot of time with someone, if you want to have a close relationship that has staying power.

WHERE TO MEET YOUR MR. RIGHT

There are particular places you can go to find eligible men, some better than others for particular types of guys, and we'll look at that in a later section. But first of all, don't forget that Mr. Right could be anywhere, because men are everywhere you go.

It's A Numbers Game

To find Mr. Right you have to meet a lot of Mr. Wrongs and if you rarely meet new guys, you are unlikely to find the guy of your dreams among the few you come across in the normal course of events.

The more guys you meet, the better it is for you. Not only will you have more chance of finding out that one of those guys is right for you, but you will also realize that you can be more choosy when it comes to selecting dates. That way, you will be less liable to grasp the first man who comes along and shows any interest.

Why does any woman put up with a guy who shows her no respect or treats her badly? Firstly, because she doesn't feel she is worth more (that's lack of confidence rearing its ugly head again) and/or secondly because she believes he might be her only chance. But if you know there are hundreds of guys out there and you are meeting new guys every week, there's no reason to settle for Mr. Not Right At All.

Chances are you don't believe me when I say there are tons of single guys out there. Every woman believes they are in short supply. And that belief seems to hold true whether she lives in the country or in a big metropolis with literally millions of guys. Just suspend your disbelief while going through this book and you will be finding those men everywhere.

Missing Men

You probably recognize logically that there are plenty of men around but because you're not interacting with them or even noticing them, and they are not approaching you, they may as well not be there.

It's time to change that.

For the next few days don't get engrossed in your smartphone, newspaper, or thoughts as you go about your day. Take notice of every male you come across. To make sure you're doing this exercise, guess the age, height and name of every guy who crosses your path. You'll never know whether you're right, but it forces you to focus on each guy you encounter for just a moment.

How many men do you come across in a typical week day or weekend that you don't normally notice? It's probably a lot more than you think. It's worth doing this exercise for that realization alone.

How To Meet Them

You may be thinking that it's all very well but you are just passing these guys on the street or seeing them in the elevator at work or at the coffee bar where you get your lunch. You don't know them, so how can that help?

The Missing Men exercise was partly just to get you to see how many men are out there. It's true you know nothing about them. Many of the men who crossed your path might be married or otherwise attached, gay or not interested for any number of reasons, and you might not be interested in them.

However, if you see guys everywhere you go and do nothing, you'll never get to meet them and find out if they are available or if there's any spark going between you. It's likely that some will have caught your eye immediately, but others could be attractive and grow on you because of their sparkling personality, intelligence, kindness and wit and you will never know that unless you get to meet them.

So what's a girl to do?

The answer is to make contact with lots of people you come across in the course of your everyday life until you get exceedingly relaxed about it. We touched on this in the Practice Talking To Strangers section above, but it bears repeating as I really can't emphasize it enough.

Don't speak only to those guys who you find attractive (though you can talk to them too). Make a cheerful comment to anyone who crosses your path. This could be the store assistant, the security guard at work, or the guy next to you in line at the coffee shop.

It doesn't have to be anything dramatic, just a comment about the weather or the traffic or the cakes on display. It can be as trite or banal as you like. Any comment shows that you're acknowledging the existence of the person you make a comment to and they in turn will know you're alive. Join the human race. We are social creatures who have had it largely knocked out of us by the busy pace of modern life so get back in the game.

Sometimes that tiny interaction will be all there is to it and the other person goes on with their day just as you will. Lots of your conversations will be with women or old guys or kids and that's fine. Other times your little comment will lead to a longer conversation with a guy you're attracted to, and if that happens you can be playful and teasing to let him know you're interested.

Either way it doesn't matter. You're expanding the number of guys you interact with in a week and that increases your odds of Mr. Right coming along without you having to go anywhere different. You just have to go about your day and keep your eyes open, then use little conversational openings with people you encounter.

Why Bother Speaking To Everyone?

You may ask why you should interact with everyone when you really only want to speak to those you're attracted to.

Think about it.

If you restrict yourself, you'll be less natural and practiced in your approaches when you make them and more concerned about the outcome. If the guy you like the looks of is the fiftieth person you spoke to this week, you'll have less trouble thinking of something to say or worrying about saying it.

This can work anywhere, so anywhere is your playground for finding Mr. Right. Play this game the whole time and enjoy the experience.

Interacting with people makes you seem friendly, approachable and charismatic. If Mr. Right catches sight of you talking to others, so much the better. He'll see you as someone with a great personality and attitude and that's a good thing, right? He might very well come closer to see if you'll talk to him too, and you will – won't you? – because it will be second nature to you after a while.

182 GREAT PLACES TO MEET MEN

Having established that you can meet Mr. Right anywhere, as you go about your normal business, I want to suggest now that you don't limit yourself to that. Sure, you'll meet more guys if you keep interacting with people as you encounter them, but you're still likely to see a limited number of new faces if you keep to the same old routine.

So here is a list of the types of places where you can exponentially multiply the number of guys you could meet and interact with. Most of these ideas give you not only places where you can meet many single guys, but they also offer ready made topics of conversation so you don't have to think too hard about what to say.

Pick out those suggestions which appeal to you because you're interested, not just because you think you'll meet the type of guys you're looking for there. Looking for a guy is not a desperate quest and nothing to be ashamed of. You're just being proactive about things you want in your life. But if you start going to places or doing activities you have no interest in just to get a guy, that does look desperate. And there should be plenty of ideas which do appeal to you, so don't worry about that.

WORKING HARD

As most of us spend a good proportion of our time either at work or getting to work, it's just as well that it's one of those places where you have a good chance of meeting a guy. Although Mr. Right may not be hanging out in your office, your work may still conjure him up!

1. Your Workplace

Despite some companies frowning on employees getting involved with each other, a lot of us (about a fifth of all married couples in the US according to a 2011 Stanford University study) met our future spouse at work. The larger the organization you work for, the easier it is to be discreet and the bigger the pool of available guys you have. As you're unlikely to change jobs simply because of the lack of men there, it's the luck of the draw whether you want to date any of your co-workers. Just check your company's exact policy first.

Even if you decide right away when you start a new job that there is no one in your company who catches your eye, be friendly with everyone and join in group activities. It never does any harm to expand your social life. Remember, co-workers have guy friends, brothers, cousins and even ex-boyfriends who may be right for you. Plus, guys at work have a habit of growing on you once you get to know them and see them performing well at work.

You have the advantage of slowly getting to know men at the office, well before you even think about dating. Conversation is easy and it's no problem to suggest a drink after work if you've been working on a joint project. Alternatively, there are often places to meet up such as at the company annual dinner/barbecue or regular social events organized by or for employees.

There's a disadvantage to meeting at work: if things go wrong with your relationship (though it's obviously not enough to put off twenty percent of the US population so make up your own mind). If worst comes to the worst and you can't take seeing your ex every day after you break up, you may have to switch jobs. You also need to keep your romance low-profile, without actually lying to co-workers. They are not stupid. Just keep affectionate behavior out of the office and stay clear of relationships between boss and subordinate as this can muddy the water and cause a lot of friction with others.

Types of guys you'll meet: Guys who have a job! This is also one of the easiest ways to meet professionals in the same line of work as you. You don't even need to restrict yourself to co-workers. You can also meet great guys in the same industry where you are working on joint projects, or those who are suppliers to your company or customers, which broadens your reach even further.

2. Commuting To Work

If you take the same route to work by public transport every day, you may find that you can get to know fellow commuters by being friendly to those you meet every day. I once had a one hour train commute each way to get to work and got to know my fellow passengers when there was a technical problem with the train. There was suddenly a sense of "We're all in this together." The journey was a lot more interesting after that day. But you don't have to wait for a problem; you can just say "hi" to those you recognize on your route and make a friendly comment on anything, such as a book or newspaper article they are reading.

If you travel by car, put an ad up at your place of work asking if anyone is interested in a car pool. You might save a bit of money, get some company and also meet new people that way.

Types of guys you'll meet: All kinds of working guys and professionals but not the super rich. They are probably going to the office in chauffeur driven cars and they generally don't do car pooling!

3. Out And About Around Your Place Of Work

Although there may be no one who catches you eye in your company, most factories, offices and shops are found near other factories, offices and shops so there will be loads of guys in the vicinity of your work place. You might find a cute guy in the parking lot, elevator or the entrance as you make your way to and from work. Or at the coffee shop where you buy your lunch, the gym near your office you use before or after work, or the bar where you go for an after work drink with your co-workers. So keep you eyes open and be ready to flirt a little. Always take a break at lunch time and go out and about to increase your opportunities. Besides, it's a great way to clear your head for work in the afternoon.

Types of guys you'll meet: All kinds of working guys. You will often find guys who work for the same kind of company as you, so you'll have something in the common.

4. Corporate Functions

If you have the chance to participate in corporate functions, then make the most of these. Work conferences, charitable events and inter-company activities are a great way to expand your network. Chat with everyone but don't get overly flirty in this environment as it will reflect badly on your professional status. You can easily swap business cards, though, with those you get along well with and who you feel are interested in you. If your company does not provide you with business cards, get some simple cards printed with your name, profession and number.

Types of guys you'll meet: You will generally meet the more senior people from organizations like yours, generally accomplished, gainfully employed, financially stable guys. As senior guys are more likely to be attached, take care not to get involved with Mr. Unavailable.

5. Business Networking Events

Business networking events geared for various professions take place in most towns and cities. Many are designed to help entrepreneurs find customers while some are about getting to know those in your industry. You'll find these meetings invaluable for expanding your social network as well as making professional contacts who can help you in your career.

Typical events have a main speaker talking about a topic of interest to the audience and after the main speech, there's often an opportunity for you to give an elevator pitch about yourself or your company. You will have a chance to network before and after the formal part of the event. Be sure to talk to as many people as you can, putting the focus on them and what they do. They will usually reciprocate and ask about you to return the favor. Be professional, friendly and approachable rather than overly flirty or sexy at this type of meeting. This is a business setting, after all. Swap business cards and either try to remember a few details of the person you met and what they are interested in, or jot these details down on the back of their card after the event.

You can use these details to contact people with information they might find interesting or helpful, and if it's a guy you enjoyed meeting you can take it from there with a slightly flirty phone call or email to see how that is received and whether he takes the opportunity to get to know you better.

Types of guys you'll meet: The main types of guys you will meet are ambitious professionals and entrepreneurs.

6. Business Seminars and Conferences

These types of events seem to be full of guys hitting on attractive women. Just take care, before you get involved, to make sure that the gorgeous guy laying on the charm is actually available. Conferences are rumored to be hotbeds of extramarital affairs.

You'll have a chance to get to know the rest of the participants during the breaks and at social events set up by the organizers. And the conference or seminar will give you a ready-made topic of conversation. If it's not that interesting, you can always ask him what brought him to the conference.

Types of guys you'll meet: Mainly businessmen and professionals at general business conferences and seminars, but also academics (at academic conferences), doctors (at medical conferences), etc.

SHOPPER'S PARADISE

Although we ladies have a reputation for loving to shop, guys have to buy stuff too. They may not drool over the latest fashions, shoes and beauty products but they do have hobbies and interests they love to shop for. And of course, single guys have to buy the usual day to day things we all need.

Having said that, you'll find all stores and all times of day are not created equal. If you're expecting to bump into an eligible guy on a Tuesday morning at the beauty counter, you'll probably have a long wait. So, with that in mind, here is a guide to the stores where you are most likely to meet a guy.

As for times, you're more likely to bump into a guy shopping on the weekend than during the week, although you may find one or two guys around lunch time and early evening on weekdays.

Shopping is great because you can simply go about visiting the stores you want to go to in any case and just look for opportunities to make contact while you are there. It takes no extra time at all and, in fact, you may get help with making purchasing decisions by talking to people as you shop and you can get done faster. If you're more proactive about the whole man seeking exercise, you can visit stores you wouldn't normally go to and see what transpires.

So which stores are best for meeting men?

7. Wherever You Can Buy The Latest Gadgets

This could be a department store tech department, a computer store or (a favorite) the Apple store in your city. In fact wherever, you find tech gadgets you'll find guys congregating. It's the equivalent of a new delivery of Jimmy Choos for us women, bright shiny objects that make us want to earn more so we can possess them all! If you like tech gadgets too you can easily make a comment about the latest attraction, or ask a question about it :"Are you thinking of getting one?" or "Do you know whether it's best to get this type or that type?" etc.

Types of guys you'll meet: The guys in these stores are generally bright and web-savvy, and may be a bit geeky, but not necessarily so. Lots of great guys love gadgets.

8. Bookstore

Although the advent of e-readers and online bookstores has caused a bit of a decline in the bookstore business, many are still alive and well and populated by guys looking for books to read for pleasure or something on their hobbies or interests.

Linger around the science fiction, murder mystery and thriller aisles (whichever you like best) and ask for recommendations or whether a particular book is any good. Also the sections on sport, computing, travel, science and business work well.

You're unlikely to find many men milling around the historical romance or needlework sections. If you only like girlie subjects and genres, you could ask a guy for recommendations for a gift for a male relative, and if your brother gets five thrillers for his birthday from your various visits to bookstores so be it.

Types of guys you'll meet: You will meet slightly nerdy, intellectual guys in book stores, the ones who actually read books rather than sit passively in front of the TV, but also those with a big interest in a particular hobby/sport etc.

9. Grocery Store

Single men have to eat and so you'll find them on their way home from work or on the weekend picking up something for dinner at the grocery store. It may seem like a strange place to meet men,

39

but supermarkets have been known to go so far as to have singles events at their stores.

The guys you meet there on a normal day may very well be attached, but if he's picking up single-size servings, it does give you a clue. The best thing to do is to be generally friendly as you go about doing your shopping, and take any pressure off approaching particular guys.

Talk to a few people, men and women alike, every time you go to the store. If you see a guy picking up an unusual item, such as an exotic fruit or vegetable, you can always ask if he's tried it before or say you wanted to try that but weren't sure how to prepare it. Or if he's buying meat, whether he thinks a particular cut is suitable for what you have in mind. He may not know. It doesn't matter. You made contact. There are all sorts of conversation points, for example

Unusual cheeses - "Where is that from again?"
TV dinners - Has he tried it before and does it actually taste as good as it looks as you've never found one yet that does?
Pizza - "That looks good - there's no such thing as a bad pizza is there? I think I'll get one too"
Produce - "Do you know how you tell if a melon/avocado (or whatever) is ready for eating?"

Types of guys you'll meet: Any single guy, but also those who love cooking. If you have a home chef in the making, you'll see him taking a bit of time to choose produce, and looking at ingredients rather than just grabbing the nearest pizza. Try various stores in your neighborhood at various times. The more upscale the store, the more upscale the guys you are likely to find.

10. The Mall

You can spend a fun couple of hours at the mall on the weekend checking out the guys shopping for whatever they want and need.

Instead of having to make a special journey to find stores that guys frequent, you can find them all in one place, a great time-saver, and after an hour or so, you can stop for a coffee. A guy with a lot of shopping bags is ripe for a friendly comment about having had a successful time shopping. Or you can just give a throwaway comment as you get your coffee: "I really need this after an hour out there."

Use the mall to check out gadget stores, bookstores, music stores, comic book stores and toy stores (some guys never grow out of their love for Star Wars, mechanical toys and model trains).

Also pay a visit to male clothing stores and departments where you will often find guys shopping alone. You can look for things for your brother/father etc. and ask opinions. Male relatives are very handy in this scenario and you can use the opportunity to be well organized by looking for gifts for every occasion coming up.

It's probably best not to pretend to have male relatives who don't exist in case anything comes of any of your approaches, but if the worst comes to the worst, you would probably be forgiven by any guy with a sense of humor (and an ego) if you explained that he caught your eye and it was the only excuse you could think of to talk to him.

Types of guys you'll meet: All kinds of single guys go shopping. Bonus: the attached ones are more likely to be visibly attached and shop with their partner.

11. Home Improvement Store

Any kind of store selling tools and supplies for home remodeling and repairs is bound to be full of guys. Though a large proportion of those guys will be attached with two kids and a mortgage, you will also find the guys who have just moved into their own place, and, in large stores that also cater to the trade market, guys who need supplies to carry out their work, for example, electric and plumping supplies or kitchens and bathrooms to be fitted. In any case, it's no problem every time you go to one of these stores to ask an opinion of a guy if you're looking for some help with what to buy. It will either lead to something or it won't.

Types of guys you'll meet: Guys who have their own place and property developers as well as some tradesmen. Just remember to check out whether they are wearing a wedding ring.

12. Farmer's Market

These are relaxed, friendly places for buying homegrown produce, and baked and canned goods made by small local companies. As you make your way between the stalls trying samples you can chat with stall holders about what they are selling. It's also an easy progression to chat to anyone visiting the same stall and say something like "Mmm - this is/looks/tastes so good. Have you tried it?"

Types of guys you'll meet: Guys interested in healthy eating and more environmentally conscious guys. Attached guys are quite likely to be visibly attached at these markets so single out those without a partner in tow.

13. Flea Markets And Estate Sales

These places are great for rooting around trying to find cool stuff for your home, and guys may have the same idea. You can ask opinions and make a comment over the things you like. And if no guys have sparked your interest ,at least you will have had an interesting hour or two. Just don't find yourself bidding by mistake for some monstrosity at a sale if you have your eye on something and decide to stay for the auction.

Types of guys you'll meet: Guys with a sense of style and history and with a place of their own to furnish, or interior decorators looking on behalf of clients.

42

14. Wine And Beer

Depending on local laws, in some places guys can pick up wine and beer along with the groceries. In others, they buy at the liquor store (called an off-license in the UK). Either way, there's an easy opening to ask advice about making the right choice among the gazillions of bottles of wine available. He may be browsing the shelves picking up a bottle of wine to take along to a party (or alas, to a girlfriend's house) or he may be buying beer for a BBQ or pizza night at home, but a throwaway spontaneous question or comment does no harm. Perhaps he'll take you along with him!

If you like making your own beer and wine, you'll find plenty of guys at the places that sell the supplies you need and you can also ask questions about the equipment and process.

Types of guys you'll meet: All kinds of guys, unlikely to be teetotalers (if that is important to you) though they may be buying wine for a gift.

IT'S A CELEBRATION

We all love a good celebration. Celebrations are meant to be happy events and everyone is out to have a good time. Not only that, but the atmosphere at these events is open and friendly. You are meant to get to know those you don't know already. The fact that a guy is there (unless he's a gate crasher) means that he's probably acquainted with someone you know, so introductions are easy. What's not to like?

Well, the downside to celebrations can be that they represent time passing for you, such as big birthday milestones, "I'm 30 and I haven't met anyone," or happy times happening for others and not you – "If I have to attend another wedding or baby shower, I'm going to scream." Plus, if it's a family event you'll get people asking the inevitable questions about whether you're still single and if it will be your turn next.

Try not to let it get you down. Go to every celebration with a determination to enjoy it and you're more likely to make the most of it and attract the attention of any single men who happen to be there. Plenty of people meet their future spouse at a friend's happy event, so it could be you. Don't forget to check out the shy guys when you go to parties, the ones on the edges of the action, rather than just those vying to be the center of attention. The shy guys often have a lot more going for them than first appears and they'll be happy to talk to you.

15. Wedding

A wedding is one of the best ways to meet a guy. Although you don't have much control over the invitations that flow your way, if you follow the advice about expanding your whole social network rather than just trying to meet men, you'll find that you are invited to quite a few. And you never know who will be on the guest list to get acquainted with. There are all those brothers, cousins, friends of the groom and of the bride, and co-workers they like enough to invite. What's more, you're all thrust together for hours of eating, drinking and dancing.

There's plenty of time to get to meet any of the guys you have your eye on as you mingle, and you have plenty of ready-made topics of conversation about how you know the happy couple, the event itself, the food, the music, or anything complimentary about the day or the couple. The whole atmosphere is one of romance. As if that wasn't enough, you'll have made an effort to look great and so will he.

Types of guys you'll meet: All kinds of guys acquainted with the bride or groom. At least you'll know they are single if they arrive alone, or you can ask whoever you both know if they are.

16. Birthday, Engagement Or Anniversary Party

These parties are generally shorter, less formal (and less romantic) affairs than a wedding but you can still meet plenty of brothers, co-workers, friends, etc., you don't know just like you can at a wedding, and again you can mingle and ask questions quite naturally without looking like you're coming on too strong with anyone. Look good, be your best sparkling self and you never know what might happen.

Types of guys you'll meet: Guys who the host/hostess is acquainted with (and at least likes well enough to invite).

17. Costume Or Halloween Party

Costume parties are always fun and you can easily start a conversation with a hot guy about his costume. The only trouble is, it may be hard to see he's hot or what he normally looks like behind his costume depending how elaborate it is. Make sure when you're choosing yours that it enhances your look rather than detracts from it!

Types of guys you'll meet: Guys who like to have fun

18. House Parties

People have parties for all sorts of reasons. Accept as many invitations as you can, whatever the event, and be sure to mingle and chat with the assembled guests. You can always ask how they know the host.

If you enjoy giving parties, have one of your own and ask your guests to bring someone you don't know so you can expand your social circle and theirs. You have a ready-made excuse to chat with everyone if you are the hostess and you can ask who they came with if you don't know them.

45

You don't even have to have a typical party. Throw a summer BBQ in your backyard, a winter snowball party or a Monday night football night in with a pot of chili and a few beers. The bonus when you give parties is that you also get invited to more parties in return.

Types of guys you'll meet: Sociable guys

FOOD & DRINK

Anywhere you find food and drink, you're likely to find people intent on consuming them, and largely a fresh crowd of people every time time you go to a new place! Whenever you go to any kind of watering hole or food place, keep your eyes open and be sociable.

The type of places you go determines the type of people you'll meet. Choose those bars and restaurants favored by the type of guys you go for. If you like city guys, the coffee shop or wine bar in the financial district of your city is a good bet, for example.

In some ways it's nice to become known in a few places in your city so you can chat to the barista, bar owner and regular customers, but if you feel like you already know everyone and you're not meeting guys you like, switch things up now and again and try a new place. You want to expand your reach!

19. Coffee Shops

Coffee shops are great places to frequent alone. You can sit with your coffee and your laptop, book or newspaper without feeling out of place by yourself. If you don't immerse yourself too much in what you're doing, being alone can make you seem more approachable than if you show up with a friend.

Every time you go to a coffee shop, make it a goal to chat with (or at least make a friendly comment to) three people. You can talk with those next to you in the line waiting for your coffee, be friendly to the barista while placing your order and comment about how busy/quiet it is or chat about the weather to the guy at the next table. If the coffee shop is crowded, you can go further and ask to share a table.

Types of guys you'll meet: All types of guys love coffee

20. Restaurants

It's not easy to meet guys at restaurants in the evenings. Basically you are usually with a friend or friends and so is he, and you're sitting at separate tables in different social groups, so you might think there's little opportunity to meet. And you'd be right most of the time. Most guys hate approaching you when there's an audience and it's probably the same for you approaching him.

At lunchtime, or early evening it may be a little easier, especially if he's just grabbing a quick bite to eat to save himself from making food at home and eating alone, so you may have more luck if you tend to do the same. You'll find him with his head stuck in a book or smartphone often at the bar rather than a table (if it's the kind of place where you can eat at the counter). If you do the same, and eat at the counter, you can chat to the server and try and bring him into the conversation.

One other way to meet men dining solo at restaurants in the evening is if you are both visiting a city on business. You are likely to find guys eating alone in the restaurant of business hotels. Chances are they may be married or live far from you, however, so proceed with caution.

Types of guys you'll meet: Professional guys, especially those who don't like to cook

21. Restaurant Events

Some restaurants hold events to help attract diners and these often have a theme and involve group seating so you can get to know other diners whether you go alone or with a friend. The theme will give you something to chat about and an interesting and more sociable evening than the usual dining experience. Look out for these events in the local press. You may find everything from grand openings and evenings based on ethnic food or special occasions to organized singles events.

Types of guys you'll meet: Sociable guys who like good food

22. Wine Tasting

Restaurants, vineyards, liquor stores and wine bars may hold special tasting evenings where you will be offered several different wines to try with some explanation of what to look for as you taste. You don't need to be an expert to enjoy a wine tasting and you may come home with a new favorite wine, if not a new friend.

The atmosphere at these events is usually quite sociable, helped, no doubt, by the wine being consumed and you can always ask about the wine and whether a guy enjoyed it or what his favorite was.

Experts recommend spitting out the wine when tasting but I never felt the need to spit any out. Just know when you have had enough and stop drinking. You don't need to drink a whole glass of every type you are offered. And get home safely. Don't drive to these events.

One thing to avoid when getting dressed is spraying on a lot of perfume as it can detract from the wine tasting experience if all anyone can smell is your Chanel No. 5.

Types of guys you'll meet: Guys who like the finer things in life and appreciate a good bottle of wine

23. City Bar Or Club

This is where single women typically go in the evenings to meet men but often end up coming home disappointed. There's a way to get the best out of the experience but it can seem a bit like a cattle market at times with many guys looking for one night stands or just out for a night with their buddies and a few laughs.

What's more, although some guys would like to meet a girl there for something longer term, the nice guys (who don't go after everything in a skirt) are frightened to approach women in case they get turned down and become a laughing stock with their buddies.

If that wasn't bad enough, it's difficult to hold a conversation and attract any guy with your sparkling personality if you can hardly hear what you're thinking, never mind what he's saying.

So, it could be a dead loss, but if you're at least average looking and are willing to flirt a bit, you can get as far as exchanging phone numbers with a nice guy.

First you have to look the part to attract the nice guys and keep the sharks at bay. And that means having the self-confidence not to rely on pure sex appeal to get noticed. If you show off a lot of flesh, you'll have guys hitting on you all night but it won't be the kind of guys who will want to take you home to meet their family in a few months time. You have to find a way to show your sex appeal without being sleazy. Keep it subtle.

Next, you need to give Mr. Nice Guy some encouragement by making it obvious you noticed him, not just by looking over once and thinking that will do. Guys are useless at recognizing that you like them from one look. Look once, let him see you looking, look

49

HOW TO FIND LOVE

away and then back again with a slight smile on your lips or a twinkle in your eye. Then during the evening find some way to separate yourself from your friends, reduce the physical distance between you and say hi to him. Nothing more. If he doesn't take up the reins then, he's not interested or he's so shy he'll never manage a conversation if you go out.

If Mr. Nice Guy turns out to have a lot more confidence than you thought, perhaps approaching you first, exercise caution because many players and pick up artists are in disguise as nice guys. They know exactly how to get your defenses down by being nice, treating you with respect, being interested in what you have to say and being confident from the get go. Genuine nice guys have had less practice at talking to women and might bungle things a bit at the start, but if you give them the benefit of the doubt their confidence will pick up.

Whatever happens, keep your wits about you and don't get drunk, because you need your defenses up and your intuition in full working order unless you just want to go home with some smooth talking guy for the night.

Types of guys you'll meet: Mainly guys looking for a good time and a few who would like to meet a nice girl like you. It's up to you to separate the wheat from the chaff.

24. Karaoke Bar

You can have a fun evening at a karaoke bar with a group of friends and have a lot of laughs and you can attract a lot of attention if you have the nerve to get up on stage. Whether you attract the right kind of attention depends on whether or not you can sing! You can always make sure you bump into and compliment a guy who sings well if you like the looks of him.

Types of guys you'll meet: Fun guys. And at least you'll know if he can sing or not!

50

25. Sports Bar/Stadium

A sports bar on a game night may be the last place you feel like going if you're not into sports, but there's bound to be some sport or other that you enjoy and can wrap your head around. Most guys like sports and a beer or two.

If you meet in a bar you get a chance to see how much he drinks, whether he gets aggressive when he has a few and his team loses, and how he relates to others such as the bartender and other customers.

If he's so into the action on the screen that he doesn't notice your existence, or respond when you make a comment, he is probably not for you, but most guys will respond as long as you don't distract them just when it gets to the crucial moment of the game.

Go with a friend, if you're shy, but not a whole big group of girls, and you'll be well outnumbered by guys. Even if you don't like sports at all, you can always just have a fun time with your friend, enjoying a few drinks and snacks and soaking up the atmosphere. Chances are guys will approach you, if you seem happy, relaxed and friendly even if you're not closely following the action.

Big football games mean lots of guys congregate in sports bars and it's a great time to catch guys if you can get interested enough to support the local team (and maybe wear the jersey). Read up a bit about the rules and you can always ask someone to explain any of the more complicated scenarios.

If you are a sports fan yourself, try going to live events wearing the jersey or colors of the local team. Baseball, basketball, football, hockey or athletic events are all good although ticket prices can dig a hole in your budget if you attend a lot of events so make the most of your time there. If you're not sitting near a hunk of a guy in the stands, get yourself something to eat or drink. Refreshment places at the stadium or ground will be chockablock with men buying beer, hot dogs and other junk food. Lines will be long and you can chat to whoever is next to you.

Types of guys you'll meet: Sociable guys that like sports.

GET SPORTY

Perhaps going to a sports bar or stadium is as sporty as you want to get, but if you enjoy participating in sports, it can be a great way to meet guys.

Sporty guys are generally more attractive than a lot of other types of guys. That's because they look after themselves. What's not to like about toned muscles, strength and fitness in a guy? The only problem might be if he admires himself just a bit too much!

26. Gym

The gym might seem like the worst place to meet men. There you are, sweating away, with your makeup all worn off, puffing and panting, red in the face and some Adonis with big muscles hits on you. Oh dear! Think of that in reverse and don't approach anyone deep into his workout. You have to pick your moments and throw a friendly comment in the direction of the guy you have your eye on at the right time. That might be before either of you get started, in the snack bar after your workout or before your class gets going or just as your instructor finishes.

As for activity, choose those classes you like that attract at least an even number of men and women, if not a better ratio, to have the most chance meeting someone, or stick with the weights room.

Conversation is easy. You can ask if he's a regular at the gym, whether he's done that class or workout before or how his workout went. You'll find making contact easier on quiet nights at the gym, the later in the week the better. Every Tom, Dick and Harry is keen to get fit on a Monday and that seems to fall by the wayside the closer to the weekend it gets.

You might think there were more options at the start of the week because of that but there will also be more competition and a large interested audience for anything you say. If you're going to the gym to keep fit 3 to 5 nights a week, you'll have lots of options and can take your opportunities as they come.

Types of guys you'll meet: Sporty types interested in staying healthy.

27. Running, Cycling or Rowing Club

If you enjoy running, rowing or cycling at the gym you can find better pickings at a club than pounding away by yourself on a treadmill, rowing machine or stationery bike. These clubs are sociable by nature and you are bound to get to know other members, many of whom will be men. In any case, the more you expand your social reach the better, so it's great to get to know the women too. Check the level of expected fitness before you join, but most clubs have a section for beginners. If not, you have an incentive to get fit before you join!

Types of guys you'll meet: Sporty guys who prefer getting fit in the company of others rather than going it alone.

28. Local Sports Teams/Community Leagues

There are many co-ed teams organized by companies and local communities where you'll be welcome to join in. Recreational sports leagues expect more enthusiasm than skill but you'll get better over time as you play and you'll naturally make friends with those on your team.

Most teams will socialize after the game with drinks or a meal and you'll soon get to know everyone. You do have to give up one

53

evening a week to do this on a regular basis, and potentially some time for extra training, but it will be well worth it to get fit, have fun and expand the number of people you know well in your city. Even if the guy of your dreams is not on your team, he may be on a opposing team or be related to or friends with someone on yours.

Types of guys you'll meet: Sociable guys who like to play team sports

29. Jogging/Fun Run

Even if you don't run in an organized group, running outdoors does have some advantages.

Joggers are generally a friendly bunch and if you choose popular places to jog such as the park or beach, you'll bump into the same guys over and over again and can easily start to say "hi" and smile whenever you come across them. Then you can start adding a brief comment such as, "How's it going today?" or something. Eventually, you're bound to end your workout at the same time (extra points for engineering that!) and have a longer chat about your training. Perhaps going for a long cool drink is in order.

If that doesn't work for you, try joining in a 5K or 10K fun run. There will be time for chatting at the start and end of the race and it's easy to find someone running at the same pace as you, and chat as you go. If you can't talk you're running too fast unless you're only there to win the race!

Types of guys you'll meet: Those who love to keep fit on a regular basis

30. Bowling

Grab a few gal pals and book a session at the bowling alley. These places are quite sociable as scoring monitors and seats are next to each other so it's easy to get a conversation started. You might not get the group of your dreams next to you, but you can have fun anyway. And if you go bowling often enough, the law of averages says you'll eventually be next to a group of cool guys. To increase your odds, take a look at the alleys before paying and request a particular alley number if you notice one free next to guys you'd like to meet.

Types of guys you'll meet: Guys of all types out having fun

31. Rock Climbing

You can learn rock climbing at an indoor center and gradually build up to going on outdoor climbs in a group. It's a sociable sport as you need a partner to practice it and classes will pair you up. As a rule, you can't choose your partner; however there should be plenty of interaction in a group class. Climbing is more popular with men than women so make the most of it!

Types of guys you'll meet: Rugged outdoor types with a sense of adventure

32. Skiing/Snowboarding

If you like to ski or snowboard then take to the slopes whenever you have the opportunity. The more experienced you are, the more daring the run you can manage and the more men/fewer women you'll find. Just make sure you have the ability before you attempt a tricky slope.

You'll have a chance to make contact while waiting for the lift to the slopes, during the day as you stop off for lunch or hot chocolate and as you come off the slopes as well as when you socialize in the evening. It's natural to swap information about the various runs and how your day turned out.

Types of guys you'll meet: Outdoor types. As skiing is not cheap, guys you meet are generally financially solvent. The more up-market the resort, the richer the guys you'll find, including European royalty. But even in the more accessible places you'll have fun and potentially meet some great guys.

33. Water Sports

There are all kinds of activities you can do on and in the water: surfing, windsurfing, sailing, water-skiing, scuba diving, kayaking, whitewater rafting and so on.

If you enjoy water sports (or think you might enjoy them) take every opportunity you can to indulge in your favorite activities even if you can only manage weekends away and vacations. So much the better if you live near the beach and can practice them regularly. A camaraderie easily builds up between those regularly practicing the same sport in the same location, as it's good to look out for each other on the water.

Take lessons if you're inexperienced so you can join in group activities and try to go for those courses which last all day or all weekend so you get a chance to interact with others while getting a solid grasp of the sport and having fun at the same time. Water sports generally have a higher percentage of guys to girls and you will have plenty to talk about with fellow participants whether you're taking a course or doing it for real!

Types of guys you'll meet: Adventurous sporty guys with a dare-devil streak

34. Golf

Golf is great for those who don't like anything too rough and dangerous. It's all about skill at an amateur level and you get to play on an even playing field with more experienced players due to the handicap system.

56

You'll need a certain level of skill, however, before going out on a course so you don't hold up everyone playing behind you. To get up to speed, you can take group or individual lessons. If you choose a group it will be more sociable and it might give you ready-made partners to play with.

Once playing, you can chat in the club house before and after the game and there's always the bar where you can meet fellow golfers. If you join a club, there may be opportunities to play competitions and tournaments where you are grouped together in a round with others. Go for mixed tournaments and see who you get to play with.

Types of guys you'll meet: Generally older guys though not exclusively. The golf course is a favorite place for many professionals and businessmen to meet out of the office

35. Martial Arts Training

Most martial arts classes are awash with guys. You have to be disciplined during the class and follow instruction but there should be a chance to chat before and after the lesson. Chatting should be easy, in the case of contact sports, if you just spent the last ten minutes of the lesson grappling with a guy!

If you prefer not to grapple, try T'ai Chi, though you will find a higher number of women and older people there for that reason. It's gentle as martial arts go.

Types of guys you'll meet: All kinds of guys seem to be attracted to these disciplines

36. Hiking

For safety's sake choose a well-populated trail and take a friend. Make sure the trail is well within your capability and that you have the right equipment. Chat with those you meet on the trail. Most people are friendly on these walks.

If you enjoy hiking, join a group which organizes events on weekends and you'll have a ready-made friendly social group to join.

Types of guys you'll meet: Rugged, outdoor types

BE AN ANGEL

Being a contributor to others can make you feel good as well as giving you the opportunity to meet lots of guys in a very natural way. You are simply working together on a joint cause and doing whatever it takes. The focus is not on you or on meeting people but on others, so it's a great way to take the pressure off if you're shy.

37. Volunteering For Charities

Volunteer work involves helping individuals or a community to achieve something they couldn't manage alone. You will generally work in a group with other volunteers and spend time doing anything from managing a homeless shelter to clearing an overgrown community garden so that everyone can benefit.

Be sure to choose a cause and activity you like and one which is done on a team to have the best chance of meeting people, although you will always get to the meet the organizers and usually those who benefit from your efforts at some point.

If you choose an activity with physical work involved such as digging ditches, clearing derelict land, building walls or decorating houses, it is likely to have a higher proportion of guys than softer activities such as visiting the old and sick. In any case, people are naturally friendly in this kind of helping environment and you'll soon get to know the other regular volunteers.

Types of guys you'll meet: Optimistic, happy guys with a giving attitude

38. Fund-Raising

With fund raising you are also making a contribution but the activities are generally mad-cap or fun activities to raise money rather than work activities which achieve a useful purpose. As far as meeting guys go, fund raising is just as helpful as volunteering. Quite often a charity where you are a volunteer may ask you to get involved in a fund-raising event and this can often be a way to break the ice even further with fellow volunteers. You can have a laugh and raise money for your favorite charity.

Types of guys you'll meet: Altruistic fun guys. Look for those guys bursting with fund-raising ideas as they are probably creative go-getters at work too

39. Community/Support Groups

Community and support groups are set up by people themselves rather than registered charities for a particular purpose. If you are naturally affected by the issue the group was designed for, you will be welcome, but it may also be appropriate for you to help out if you have moved on beyond an issue you used to have. Your experience can be invaluable.

You will find groups that cover things like addiction, support for victims of crime, single parents support, parents of drug users, support for carers or a phobia group. You can find groups in your area with an online search.

If you need support, you need to focus on that rather than meeting new people, but you can find good friends going through similar experiences in these groups, not necessarily romantic relationships. Remember every friendship expands your network, and your good friends will know other people. Among them you might find the guy for you.

Types of guys you'll meet: Most likely a guy you meet in a group like this is going to have an issue to work through or a set of circumstances which are not ideal. A single parent or guy with an issue may still be right for you. Just exercise caution if you always seem to fall for guys with problems in your romantic relationships.

40. Member Of The Board

If you serve on the board of an organization, you will get to know fellow board members during the course of meetings and there will be an opportunity to talk socially before and after the meeting. Look for opportunities to serve in areas of special interest to you, if you have time on your hands and relevant experience.

Types of guys you'll meet: You will generally find older and professional guys on boards, with a mix of married and divorced guys.

41. Protest Meetings

If you care strongly about a particular issue, turn up at protest meetings. You can be sure of bumping into those of similar views, the people who care passionately about them.

I'm not talking about getting involved in anything where the consequences of the protest can have serious repercussions on your life (like arrest, etc.) simply to meet a man. If you're serious enough about a cause to risk something like like that, you're probably already involved anyway. But it does no harm to lend your support for the things you care about, such as turning up to town meetings to protest about environmental issues.

Types of guys you'll meet: Earnest guys willing to take action about things they believe in.

SPIRITUAL PURSUITS

If you have a religious belief and regularly attend a place of worship, you will often find there are social activities organized which are designed for people of similar beliefs to get to know each other.

42. Religious Services

Talking during a service is frowned upon, but there may be an opportunity to say "Hi!" before or after the service if male/female interaction is encouraged in your religion. Most of those attending religious services will be open and friendly so you are unlikely to get a scowl in return. If you attend regularly and haven't seen a particular guy before, you can ask if he's new in the area. If you attend a new place of worship for the first time, you can ask if he usually goes to that service.

Types of guys you'll meet: Men practicing the same faith as you

43. Organized Events

Take part in as many of the social events attached to your place of worship as you can but especially those where the particular activity interests you. This way you'll have fun, as well as getting to know the people in your community: young, old, male and female. People seem to love to matchmake when it comes to getting two people of the same faith together, so you can expect to be introduced to a number of men by getting to know everyone socially.

Types of guys you'll meet: Men practicing the same faith as you

HAVE FUN LEARNING

This is one of my favorite ways to meet guys, but then I'm bound to be in favor, as I met my husband at college! The great thing about meeting in this way is that it doesn't matter how old you are. You are never too old to learn something new!

44. College

Many couples first get together at college. It's one place you can guarantee you'll meet people where almost everyone is single, intelligent, intent on learning/pursuing a good career, as well as out to have a good time.

No one should be choosing a career or major subject because of the number of men also pursuing it, but it's a fact that some courses are more heavily weighted to men than others, making it easier to meet men naturally while attending classes. If you choose subjects like languages or nursing that are heavily favored by women, try to include some options or modules that attract plenty of men too.

That is not to say that you have to meet men during actual classes. There are plenty of ways to bump into guys on campus. You'll find them at the library, in the coffee shop, or waiting in line at lunch places. You'll also find them at places just outside the campus, for example, at the laundromat, gym, and grocery store.

As part of college social activities, you'll see plenty of guys at student parties, college sports training/matches and at the events organized by interest based groups that all colleges have.

Types of guys you'll meet: Guys with potential in all sorts of careers, as well as intellectuals and academics

45. Back To School

Local community colleges and universities offer courses in all kinds of subjects so you can join a learning environment long after you left school far behind. If you don't want to take an academic course, there are night classes on all kinds of subjects available, from silver jewelery making to cupcake decoration, from landscaping to computer studies. Simply pick up the listings and see what you'd like to do, then enroll.

When choosing a course that will help you meet men, pick one that is likely to have more male participants than females and one where you will be forced to interact rather than sit behind a desk: for example, "Basic Cookery for One" (where you will share equipment with a partner), "Spanish for Business" (where you need to talk to each other in Spanish) or "Video Production 101" (where you will create a group project) might work for you. Ask for details about how the course is run before you enroll.

If you take a new course every couple of months, you'll have fun, increase your knowledge and make tons of new friends of both sexes.

If you want to expand the number of courses to choose from, also look for independent courses run by cookery or language schools, photographers or picture framers and similar types of small businesses near your home or place of work.

Types of guys you'll meet: Guys interested in the same subjects you are.

46. Learn A Foreign Language

You can take languages classes at community college but one of the best ways to learn a language (if you have the basics) is with a conversational group. You will naturally get to know the others in the group while you talk.

You can either start one (advertise on Craigslist for a native speaker and participants) or join an existing group if you know of one.

Or you can practice your language one to one by advertising for a language partner who wants to improve English at the same time as you improve your foreign language.

Your language partner is probably not the guy of your dreams but is more likely to become a new friend and help expand your social circle into an entirely different set of people.

If you can afford it, an immersion course in the foreign country related to your language is a great way to meet people from all over the world, but you're unlikely to meet a partner who lives close to you. For meeting guys, it would be better to take an intensive business level language course in your city, and hope Mr. Right is not taking the course because he's about to be sent overseas.

Types of guys you'll meet: Intelligent guys interested in learning the same language as you

CULTURE VULTURE

If you love art, literature, film or music of any kind, then there are plenty of places in most cities to find guys who have the same kind of interests as you. Subscribe to a local newspaper or listings magazine so that you know exactly what is on when. You'll find all kinds of concerts, stand-up comedy shows, exhibitions, movies, festivals, readings and openings listed.

47. Art Galleries And Museums

Most towns and cities have an art gallery with both permanent and visiting exhibitions. Keep an eye out for events happening at your local gallery and visit in the evening or the weekend when working guys are more likely to be around.

Take your time to check out both the pictures and the visitors and you can talk to anyone you like about the exhibits. An opening question like, "What do you think of this?" or "Is this the same artist who painted...?" is enough to get things started and he can take it from there if he likes.

You may also find commercial exhibitions and art fairs where the artwork is for sale. Don't worry, you don't have to purchase anything but you will see some interesting work from new artists and there is often more to say about that!

Types of guys you'll meet: Guys who appreciate art, and perhaps an artist or two.

48. Book Readings

If you visit a book festival you'll find many book readings in one place over a few days or you can look for events held by your local bookstore.

After the reading, people will hang around to buy the book and get it signed by the author so there should be an opportunity to ask any good-looking guy what he thought of the reading and whether he's read anything else by the author or something similar.

Types of guys you'll meet: Intellectual guys and thinkers who like to read

49. Film Festival

Apart from the big, well-publicized film festivals in places like Cannes, you may find smaller film festivals showing movies with a particular theme closer to home. Although there's no chance to chat or meet anyone during the movie, you may have the opportunity to comment and smile when you collect your tickets, buy drinks or leave the auditorium. And the more interesting the movie, the more you'll have to say.

Types of guys you'll meet: Those interested in the same genre of movies as you

50. Outdoor Movie, Play Or Concert

In the summer months, you'll find all kinds of cultural events taking place outdoors in places where the weather is reliable (and even where it's not).

The idea with many of these events is that you sit and watch the movie or play or listen to the concert at the same time you enjoy the fresh air and often a picnic. If it's a "sit on the grass and picnic" type of event, go with a few friends taking a potluck picnic and drinks.

Everyone brings too much so you can always share with those nearby. Choose your position carefully so you're next to a mixed group with guys to spare. It's not the kind of thing guys go to on their own to meet women. If you bring cold beer and bar snack type food, it will be especially popular with guys.

Types of guys you'll meet: Cultured guys, usually in groups including both men and women. Try not to tread on another girl's toes

51. Rock Festival

An entirely different kind of cultural event, a rock festival is outdoors but you will be standing in a huge crowd rubbing shoulders with everyone else. These events of full of guys and are generally for the young, although you will find guys of all ages there who are young at heart. You're likely to find yourself sleeping in a tent on site, knee deep in mud if the weather takes a turn for the worse (take your waterproof boots) and standing in line to use the bathroom (take your own paper supplies).

If you can stand that kind of thing, and can live without your curling iron, you'll have great fun, enjoy the music and will be surrounded by thousands of guys for a whole weekend.

Types of guys you'll meet: Young guys (or the young at heart) who like that kind of music

52. Music Club/Watching Bands

Similar to a music festival, but without the mud and tents, you can meet a great guy at any live music venue. Choose smaller concerts for more opportunity to chat and meet people. Those venues are generally more intimate and it's easier to move around and mingle.

Plenty of guys go to watch bands alone because it's their type of music and their taste is not shared by their friends. And being alone means he's likely to welcome some company.

Types of guys you'll meet: Similar to rock concerts, you'll find young guys (or the young at heart) who share your taste in music. You may also find yourself mingling with the band at smaller venues.

53. Choir

Joining a choir can give you a chance to meet a whole new set of people. If you can sing and enjoy using your voice, investigate what is available. Many choirs are linked to places of worship but there are also choirs you can join just for fun. There should be a chance to chat before and after practice and performances, and you can always suggest going for a coffee or a drink to encourage the group to be more sociable.

Types of guys you'll meet: Avid singers, mature guys

54. Guitar Class

Look for group lessons in the music genre you love whether that is jazz, rock, pop, or classical. These classes are more popular with guys than women.

Types of guys you'll meet: Guys of all ages seem to want to take up the guitar.

OUT AND ABOUT

You may not need to do anything special to meet the guy of your dreams if you're out and about a lot going about your normal business and not sitting at home, so don't ignore the guys you meet in the course of your normal day.

Be open and friendly and talk to as many people as you can. Remember, if you have your head stuck in a smartphone, and you're constantly surfing, emailing or tweeting, you are shutting people out. You are also not noticing the guys around you. Don't get so immersed in what you're doing or thinking that you are lost to the world.

55. Eat Lunch Out

On fine days, instead of eating a sandwich at your desk, take your lunch outside and eat it sitting on a bench in the park. If the weather is bad, have a bite to eat in the corner cafe a few days a week. Getting away from your desk and going outside gives you many more opportunities to bump into guys in the elevator, coffee shop or store. If Mr. Right was going to arrive at your desk, you'd have noticed him already.

Types of guys you'll meet: Working guys of all kinds

56. Local Guys

If you don't know the people on your street or in your immediate local area, start getting acquainted! Never miss a chance to join in community events taking place such as street parties, celebrations, festivals, yard sales and fairs. And if you feel up to it, you could get to know everyone who lives nearby by organizing a community or charitable event. You'll have an excuse to talk to and invite anyone you like.

Types of guys you'll meet: Affluent guys in affluent neighborhoods, less affluent guys in less affluent neighborhoods

57. Walk The Dog

If you go for a walk in the park with your dog on a regular basis, you'll often end up on nodding terms with those who do the same. Borrow a dog if you don't have one. You will find owners who are pleased to get out of that daily walk!

Dogs are a great ice-breaker as you can always ask an owner about his dog. It doesn't seem forward, just friendly.

And there's no need to limit yourself to the park. You can walk your dog anywhere great guys hang out and the dog owners among them may very well talk to you, especially if you make a passing comment.

Try walking your dog in the business district of your city around lunchtime or early evening, or stroll past the gym, fire station or hospital for a nice mix of passers by. Just remember to take a pooper scooper and plastic bags so you can do your bit to keep the sidewalks clean.

Types of guys you'll meet: Dog lovers

58. Public Park

Local parks are not just for walking the dog. When the weather is fair, grab a friend and a soccer ball, Frisbee, or kite and spend some time messing around and watching the world go by. You can always "accidentally" run into a cute guy or kick your ball in his direction. He won't be able to resist kicking it back.

Types of guys you'll meet: Dog walkers, joggers and all types of guys just passing through on their way somewhere

59. Washing The Car

Guys love their cars so you'll find them lovingly caring for their vehicles. You can meet them waiting around at the car wash while you get yours clean at the same time.

Types of guys you'll meet: Guys with their own wheels

60. Laundromat

Even if you have laundry facilities at home, it's worth a trip to the laundromat now and then to see who's around. Take the bigger items that are easier to wash in a big commercial machine than at home, items like washable duvets, blankets, sofa covers and curtains, and you can spring clean your home at the same time.

Types of guys you'll meet: Single and newly divorced guys (who gave up access rights to the family washing machine!)

61. Public Transit

You may meet the love of your life anytime you're going from point A to B by bus, train, trolley or subway, so keep your eyes open, be friendly and choose who you sit or stand next to!

Types of guys you'll meet: All types in big cities because public services are more convenient than driving; in smaller towns the more financially challenged (no money for a car?)

62. Follow That Man!

No need to turn into a stalker but if you spot someone you like while out and about, it does no harm to take five minutes and see where he goes, without obviously following him. If he goes for a coffee, you can grab one too. If he pops into a grocery store, go and buy a loaf of bread or something and say a few words. Going after him into one place is enough, though. Don't start following him all around town. That would just be weird.

Types of guys you'll meet: All types

FAR AND WIDE

They say that travel broadens the mind, but it also broadens the amount and diversity of people you meet.

If you can afford the time and money to get away, even if it's just for a weekend, make the most of it. Most travelers are friendly and happy to talk about their experiences and it's easy to ask questions when you know very little about a place.

63. Getaways For Singles

A number of companies organize trips for single travelers, so these may be worth considering if you have spare cash. It has to be said that a lot of the vacations to romantic sounding destinations and those with comfortable accommodations are mainly taken by women, so you have to think about the things that men like to do and choose those options to have the best chance of meeting a great guy. Look for trips that involve roughing it a bit (more adventure than rest and relaxation) and those which focus on sports such as sailing or scuba diving. Climbing Mount Kilimanjaro is bound to give you richer pickings than a spa break in Switzerland though you might not enjoy it quite so much!

Types of guys you'll meet: Financially stable guys who like to travel

64. Backpacking

If you have the ability and financial wherewithal to take six months to a year off, go on an extended trip around the world and you are bound to bump into like minded travelers to swap tips and itineraries with. Travelers often hook up with others for parts of their journey (not necessarily romantically), so you are bound to meet friends and have the time of your life.

Types of guys you'll meet: Generally young carefree guys on a gap year before or after college

65. Planes And Trains

You never know who you will be sitting next to when it comes to any kind of long distance travel and it's easy enough to say a few words without being intrusive and annoying if he doesn't want to talk. If it turns out he's happy to chat, you'll have a chunk of time to get to know him before you arrive at your destination.

Ask for a middle seat in a row of three so you're less likely to be seated with a couple. Also, airports and train stations are full of coffee shops where you can while away the time before your flight or train departure and talk to other passengers.

If you don't find yourself talking to anyone on the plane, you might find someone to chat with while you're waiting for your baggage on arrival.

Types of guys you'll meet: Businessmen (take care in case he's married), college guys on the way to/from home, guys who like to travel

IT'S WHO YOU KNOW

The majority of real world relationships begin with the help and influence of people you know, so meeting men is often a function of who you know (or who is acquainted with the people you know). Remember that theory about the six degrees of separation where you are only six people in a chain away from someone who knows someone who knows any single person on the planet including all celebrities. This means you are just six degrees of separation from any single eligible man out there too!

66. Family and Friends

Tell people you know that you're ready to meet someone, especially if you've been out of the dating game for a while. That way they are more likely to introduce you to the guys they know when you're out together. They may also think of guys they know who may be right for you and invite you to the same events. You have an easy conversation opener with these guys. You can find out how they know the person who introduced you.

Because so many couples meet through mutual acquaintances, do all you can to expand your circle of friends of both sexes. If you only see three people regularly, your circle of "friends of friends" is going to be pretty limited.

Any of the activities in this book can result in making a friend or two, even if you don't meet a great guy, so make the most of whatever you do by getting to know all kinds of people.

Never worry about going to an activity or event alone, because that almost forces you to talk to others and you are more likely to make a friend that way, and if the guy of your dreams is there, it will be easier to make friends with him too.

Types of guys you'll meet: Guys of all types where you know someone in common

67. Blind Dates

Blind dates make most of us groan, usually because we have the memory of being set up by a friend with some guy who is not right for us at all and sitting through an agonizing evening knowing our friend is expecting us to report back favorably on what we thought of him.

But not every blind date is a failure and if you insist on doing some kind of fun activity rather than sitting over dinner for three hours with someone you may have nothing in common with, you can at least have a good time and a few laughs while seeing if he's right for you.

Types of guys you'll meet: Guys your friends think are just right for you

68. Neighbors

If you don't know your neighbors and you haven't lived in your place long, knock on their doors and introduce yourself. Make sure you do this whenever someone new moves in too.

If you've lived there for ages and are on nodding terms with your neighbors already but you'd like to get to know them (or at least one of them) better, invite all your neighbors for drinks one evening after finding out when most of them (including the one you're interested in) can make it.

Types of guys you'll meet: The neighbor you've had your eye on

69. Men From The Past

Think of all the men you have had some kind of contact with over the past ten years or so, for example neighbors, friends who moved away, classmates, coworkers, and friends of friends. When you met in the past, the time wasn't right for some reason. You were on the rebound or he was. He wasn't ready for a girlfriend. You had a different idea about potential in a mate in those days. Maybe he was too immature for you or didn't make an impression on you for some reason. But ten years later things could have changed - a lot.

Look these guys up, and see if they now have potential. It's simple enough to find people these days on Facebook, Google or Friends Reunited and guys are generally happy to hear from you (unless you were the girlfriend from hell!)

You can get in touch with old flames too. If you just grew apart or moved away, or he got scared you were getting too serious too soon or something like that, and years have gone by, you may have a new flame in the making.

Just don't contact any guy who had major character or personality flaws that are unlikely to have changed. For example, avoid abusers, addicts and anyone who promised to leave his wife for you and didn't. It's asking for trouble to re-open old wounds there.

Types of guys you'll meet: Ones you already know. Bonus: no getting to know you awkwardness as you already know them

70. School Reunions And Alumni Associations

This is a great way to make contact with lots of guys from your past all in one day. You can also see what a lucky escape you had with some of those you had a crush on and never got together with!

Types of guys you'll meet: Old classmates exactly the same age as you or those who studied at the same time as you

71. Just Good Friends

Perhaps you're searching far and wide for Mr. Right and missing out on the guy who is sitting right there under your nose. Could that guy who treats you like a buddy actually be the one?

Maybe you've discounted him for so long hat you miss the obvious. You think there's no chemistry there because he never treats you like a girlfriend, but that may be because you never act in a way that makes him see you as a sensual woman.

If you keep falling for bad guys, unavailable guys and guys that are plain mean, chances are that your good friend Mr. Nice isn't floating your boat right now. But it may be you should re-think that idea.

Isn't it about time you thought about what you really want? And what you really want certainly isn't a guy who ignores you, forgets your birthday and treats you badly.

Now there's a whole lot more involved in going from a just good friends relationship to something more but it's a thought anyway in covering all bases in your quest for Mr. Right.

Types of guys you'll meet: Good friends with potential for more

HOBBIES AND INTERESTS

If you want someone who's going to share your interests, then what better way to meet him than actually doing those things that interest you? And not doing those things that don't. Or to put it another way, if golf bores you to tears then don't try and meet the love of your life at a golf course or you only have yourself to blame if you become a golf widow and lose him for hours every weekend while he plays.

So just go about doing what you love and talk to anyone and everyone who enjoys the same things. Here are a few suggestions for the type of interests that many guys have to get the ball rolling and a few options for meeting people with all kinds of interests.

Just because you haven't thought about some of these pastimes up to now, doesn't mean that they can't become favorites of yours. You just need to have a genuine interest and not pursue an activity simply for the sake of meeting men.

72. Archaeological Digs

If you are the kind of girl who is happy knee deep in mud, digging in the dirt, you might have fun and meet a lot of guys working in a group as a volunteer trying to dig up evidence of the past.

Taking part will depend on whether there's anything like this going on in your local area, but it's also a great way to combine a trip abroad with an interest in archeology. Just do a search on Google for something like "archaeological digs volunteers" and you'll find plenty of options.

Types of guys you'll meet: Rugged outdoor types interested in history and not afraid to use their muscles

73. Battle Reenactment

There are all kinds of historic battles being reenacted by those with a interest in history, so if you're interested, it's worth taking a look at what is available within reach (geographically or financially).

Some of the bigger battles, for example Gettysburg, attract around 40,000 re-enactors of which the majority are men. There has to be someone for you among that kind of crowd if you have an interest in history in common.

Take a look at the information online and see if an event like that is something you could see yourself enjoying.

Types of guys you'll meet: Guys from all walks of life who love history

74. Classic Car Rallies

Guys love cars and those who like classic cars love their cars even more.

If you have a classic car yourself you can join in the rally and will get a lot of attention from guys. If you have the cash it might be worth buying a car just for that!

If you don't have the car or the cash, you can be a spectator instead.

Types of guys you'll meet: Guys with an appreciation for vintage wheels, and probably the finer things in life

75. Racing

All kinds of racing ,whether motor racing or horses or dogs seem to attract guys in their droves. Is it the danger? Is it the speed? Is it the chance to place a bet? Who knows. But it's a great place to find guys. Speedway, NASCAR, Formula One, Derby, whatever form racing takes, they are there. Ask them who they think will win or if they have had a bet on the result.

Types of guys you'll meet: Different types of racing attract different types of guys. The Grand Prix at Monte Carlo has a different crowd from horse racing but check out a few places and you'll soon see the kind of guys there and whether they are for you.

76. Conventions, Exhibitions And Trade Shows

There are all kinds of conventions and trade shows taking place all year round and it's a good idea to attend those that interest you in your region.

There are some conventions there are particularly appealing to guys such as comic-con and science fiction, video gaming or computer type conventions as well as things like car and boat shows.

If that type of thing interests you, go and meet the guys who are interested in the same things as you. If all those things leave you cold then you may still meet a few guys at more female friendly shows such as those dealing with home decoration or cookery but the competition will be higher too!

Types of guys you'll meet: Guys interested in whatever the convention is about

77. Museums

There are all kinds of museums around, not just stuffy ones full of pieces of broken pot from 12AD. Some of the best are science museums (the type where you can interact with the exhibits), observatories, space and war museums which attract a lot of guys, and open air museums which have whole villages preserved in a particular time period.

Because there's a lot to look at, you can usually start a conversation with whoever you bump into quite easily, just by commenting on one of the items on display.

Types of guys you'll meet: Intelligent guys with an interest in science or history

78. Mensa Meeting

If you have a high IQ (over 140), you might like to join a Mensa group as you'll find plenty of men there who won't be worried you're more intelligent than they are. You'll have plenty of stimulating discussions that the rest of us wouldn't have a hope of understanding, and very bright children too, no doubt, if you end up being parents together!

Types of guys you'll meet: Guys with genius level intelligence

79. Chess Club

At a chess club, you'll also meet intelligent men but chess is more accessible to people of average intelligence even though those who play at the highest level could probably give Mensa members a run for their money. Chess works well as a way to get to know people as it is a game for two and you will naturally talk to your "opponent."

Types of guys you'll meet: Intelligent, reasonably sociable guys

80

80. Geocaching

Geocaching is like a scavenger hunt where you use navigation skills to find "treasure" in your local area. Look for organized events and see if you can "team up" with someone and have fun hunting down the treasure together.

Types of guys you'll meet: Guys who like a challenge

81. Meetup Groups

Meetup groups are advertised online and are a way to find people with similar interests to you to meet up with offline. The most well known site that gathers together all kinds of meetup groups is meetup.com. You can find groups for almost anything you are interested in and also groups all over the world.

You can usually see profiles of group members so you can check to see the makeup of the group before you join. Most people going to meetup groups are interested in getting to know those with similar interests, so you will find that meetings are friendly. If you turn up on a regular basis, you will easily feel part of the group.

If there's not a meetup group in your area covering the things you are interested in, why not start one?

Types of guys you'll meet: Guys with an interest in common with you

JUST FOR SINGLES

Matchmaking of one kind or another goes back to ancient times, and although the format has changed over the centuries, it still involves getting singles together who might not otherwise meet or get together with each other.

And it still works!

Don't turn your nose up at some of the obvious ways to meet more men, just because they are obvious. If you think it seems a bit desperate to make it clear that you want to find someone, be comforted by the fact that every person involved in these activities is looking for a partner too.

What's more, so many people use these methods that's there's nothing unusual these days about meeting in this way. About 20 percent of all new marriages started on an online dating site, for example.

Also, remember that you don't need to use these methods exclusively. You can simply use them to supplement and increase the number of guys you're meeting by other methods. And, as you know, the more guys you meet, the more likely you are to find a guy who is exactly right for you.

82. Online Dating

You can find the love of your life online, just as 20 percent of adults do these days, by going about the whole process with a positive mindset, putting some effort into how you present yourself online and making the effort to meet a wide range of guys.

Online dating feels strange because you go on a date before you know if there's any chemistry and then it's either there or it's not. It's almost as if there's an extra step before the first one you'd take if you were meeting guys in person. In real life, you find out if there's any chemistry before agreeing to meet. With online dating you find out on the first date.

Never mind, you can still have fun with online dating, if you organize dates you will enjoy rather than sitting through long dinners or even coffee with someone you'd never have agreed to date if you'd met him in a bar or at work.

Suggest an activity you'd like to do such as ice skating or even something you'd normally do so you don't use up a lot of extra time such as taking the dog for a walk, and just see how you get along. It's easier to talk and get to know a guy when you're doing something active, rather than just sitting across the table from him.

Don't get excited about any profile until you meet and get to check him out for real, and you'll have far less disappointment with online dating. See it as a bit of a numbers game: the more guys you meet, the closer you get to a guy who is right for you.

Types of guys you'll meet: All types - you can choose which types of guys you want to meet from their profiles

83. Online Meets Offline

Some women have had success by having cards printed up with their profile picture and name and the website address of their online dating profile page and handing these cards out to guys they'd like to date when they come across them.

It takes some guts to do it and if you're up for that it might actually be easier just to start a conversation. That way he will show if he's interested in you right away and he doesn't have the barrier of going on a dating site he may be unfamiliar with!

It does seem like you're putting all your cards on the table (literally) when there's no need to, but there could also be occasions where there's no chance to chat and just slipping him a card would be all that you have time to do.

Types of guys you'll meet: Ones you like the looks of

84. Personal Ads

It seems strange that personal ads still exist in newspapers and magazines in the age of online dating, especially when those publications often have their own dating sites, but they are still alive and well. It's probably because they still bring in revenue from those who would rather not put their profile on an online dating site.

You can place an ad or answer one. Placing the ad is often free but it usually costs money (via a premium rate telephone service) to retrieve messages that people have left for you and to follow those messages up. And leaving a message for an advertiser usually costs money too.

Types of guys you'll meet: All types. They often have to pay per message left or send a letter so you don't get too many time wasters.

85. Speed Dating

Speed dating events are organized in many cities, usually in a bar or restaurant. You sign up and pay a fee. Sometimes drinks are included in the price. Organizers arrange seats in pairs and you get to meet each guy at the event in turn (usually 15 to 30 guys) for just a few minutes before a buzzer sounds and you get to meet the next. It's fairly anonymous as there's a system for each of you to note whether you'd like to see the other again without having to say anything face to face. The organizers collect your results at the end of the night and you'll be told after the event who wanted to see you again of those guys you met.

If you're not generally an instant hit with guys, it can be a bit demoralizing, as first impressions are what count. You don't get much of a chance to get your personality across, but at least you get to see if there's any chemistry at all before you say whether you'd like to see someone again.

On the plus side, if you tend to be picky about guys, it's a way to meet a lot of them in short succession.

Types of guys you'll meet: Most events are aimed at particular age groups with a cutoff around 40

86. Dating/Introduction Agencies

An old fashioned marriage bureau may be the answer to finding the perfect partner if you have cash to spare. It helps if you're in the under 45 age bracket as most eligible men still want a partner who is in a younger age bracket than they are.

You will have an interview to see if you are suitable to be taken on as a client and you'll be shown profiles of those that the agency thinks might be a good match for you. Good agencies also proactively look for suitable partners for you, both online and offline, if they don't have many suitable guys on their books.

The problem with this type of arrangement is the high cost and sometimes the low numbers of suitable matches. Women are more tempted to use this method than men. It's important to check the kind of numbers that you can expect to be introduced to before you sign up and pay your money.

Types of guys you'll meet: Usually well-vetted eligible guys as professional agencies go through a rigorous selection process; some agencies specialize in different types of guys, usually the most eligible in various fields

87. Singles Events

Never worry about going to a singles event alone. Essentially, everyone there is in the same boat.

You can find out about these events in the local newspaper or online (some meetup events are set up specifically for singles too).

You will find many different types of activities for singles (for example, dances, cruises and book groups) plus some that are organized by businesses to bring in customers (I've heard of these in bowling alleys, supermarkets and gyms).

You'll also find non-specialized singles social groups and clubs which get together for all kinds of activities. Many of them have a focus on making friends and expanding your social network, not just on meeting partners, and this is ideal for finding new friends if you move to a new area.

If you want to make sure you meet new people and don't just hug a glass or a corner all evening, volunteer to help at a singles evening and you'll have a good excuse to chat with everyone.

Types of guys you'll meet: All kinds of singles

NOT JUST DATING ONLINE

Even though online dating is extremely popular, you can also meet guys online without going anywhere near an online dating site.

There are people all over the Internet who share something in common with you and there are ways to get to know them. One drawback is that many will live some distance from you, but on many sites and forums there's a place to put your location so you can get to know those who live relatively close to you geographically. For those at some distance away, you may find an opportunity to meet at some time in the future, if friendship blossoms.

Do take care when meeting with anyone offline who you only know via a website. Until you know he's exactly who he says he is and you know you can trust him, don't take risks with your own safety.

88. Social Networking Sites, Forums, Groups, Chat Rooms And Message Boards

You'll find lots of places to interact online for those interested in every subject on the planet and also for all kinds of social groups. It doesn't take much to join in the thread on a particular topic and get talking. Offer your opinions, advice and sympathy and be seen as a person who is open to engaging with others about the various topics covered by the site.

Although discussions start off as public (at least between members of the group, if not the whole web) there is often a private messaging system so you can continue a discussion or ask a question away from prying eyes. For example, if a guy seems to know a lot about something you need advice on, you can ask a question privately.

Any relationship would have to develop naturally from discussions, as these sites are not meant for dating and so getting to know someone is likely to be a long drawn-out process. Sometimes members of the group will arrange online conference calls or even offline meetings and then you can get to know people more quickly.

You may find chat rooms, Google hangouts and similar forums linked to the sites you are already familiar with, and these can help forge closer relationships between members of a group.

Types of guys you'll meet: Guys who share your interests (but not always your interest in dating)

89. Online Gaming

If you like playing video games online, there are lots of opportunities via online gaming communities to play with enthusiasts from around the world, and the majority are male.

If you don't like video games, you'll find the whole thing (and probably the guys who play a lot of these games) pretty dull, so stay away if that's the case!

If you get chatting with anyone in the community, find out who you are speaking to and get his age right away or your could find you're talking to a 14 year old. Although many games are meant for the 18 plus crowd, a lot of players are younger than the age guidelines.

Types of guys you'll meet: Online gaming enthusiasts only

A GIRL'S JUST GOTTA HAVE FUN

Some of the best places to meet guys are where you'd go to have a good time whether guys were there are not. You can enjoy yourself with your friends and if a nice guy happens to come along, so much the better, but it won't spoil your day if he doesn't.

90. Beach

Hanging around at the beach in summer (or even getting bundled up and watching the crashing waves along the boardwalk in the off season) has to be one of life's great pleasures. It's something to do with all that fresh sea air.

If you live near a beach, make the most of it. In summer, put on your swimsuit or shorts and park yourself near the snack bar to catch passing "traffic." If you're feeling active (and the water's warm enough) go for a swim when you spot a great guy in the waves or ask to join in a game of volleyball.

If you prefer to be fully dressed when you meet a new guy, try jogging along the water's edge before work or at sunset, or walk your dog along the shore (if allowed).

Types of guys you'll meet: Surfers, joggers, guys relaxing at the weekend, and guys on vacation.

91. Casino

Hit the casino for a lot of glitz and glamor but make sure you don't lose your rent money! Find out what you're doing before you go if you don't know how to play. Start out with something simple like Blackjack if you're a beginner.

Though this could be an expensive way to meet men, it can be fun, and men tend to outnumber women. Not only that, but you can choose where to sit and make sure that you are next to a guy you'd like to get to know before staking any money at all.

Types of guys you'll meet: It depends on the casino but at the better casinos in major cities, you'll find well-dressed, usually mature and financially stable men. Just make sure he's not addicted to gambling. At vacation hot spots, you'll find all types of guys out for a good time.

92. Amateur Dramatics

If you join a drama group, you'll meet a whole set of new friends and have plenty to do on spare evenings. In fact, the pressure to give up your spare time will get quite intense the closer the group gets to staging a production.

If you're not so good at acting you can stick with walk-on parts or help out with lighting, music, scenery, etc. You'll get to know everyone quite well and have fun at the post production party.

Types of guys you'll meet: Mainly confident extroverted men who love acting

93. Amusement Park

This is a fun place to meet because everyone is out to have a good time and is generally having one! You'll find plenty of groups of guys at amusement parks, especially the ones with the scariest rides and longest queues.

If you like those types of rides, you can join them in the queue and start chatting, otherwise go for the tamer ones and you can meet guys when it's time for a snack or a beer.

Types of guys you'll meet: Younger guys in groups at the parks with the big rides, single dads at family parks

94. Social Dancing

If you have two left feet, join a dance class and get some lessons. Dance classes are often populated by more women than men but at least you'll be prepared to get out on the dance floor for real.

Some dances naturally lend themselves to meeting people, especially folk dancing, square dancing, Scottish country dancing and similar dances. If you love dancing, try all types until you find one with enough potential partners to keep you happy. Try salsa, ceroc, sirocco, line, swing, flamenco, or ballroom and see how you do.

Types of guys you'll meet: Guys who love to dance (or who know it's a great way to sweep a girl off her feet)

88 MORE PLACES

Apart from all the places we've already mentioned, there is a whole heap of places that might work for you to meet the man of your dreams, so see if there is anything here that you'd like to try, find out where you can do it, and give it a whirl.

They say that "feint heart never won fair lady," but "feint lady never won fair heart" either ,so get yourself out there. There's no need to stalk him. You could just bump into him doing whatever you are doing, but at least give fate a chance by getting off your sofa.

1. Volunteer for a political party
2. Play golf for a charity tournament
3. Attend free lectures at colleges/libraries
4. Become a member of Rotary
5. Join Toastmasters
6. Go to a Parents Without Partners Group (if you are a single mother)
7. Join a tennis club that organizes singles round robins
8. Hang out with single male friends and get to know their friends
9. Fly a kite and look like you need help
10. Attend book readings for thriller or sci-fi writers
11. Join a photography club
12. Attend charity dinners
13. Volunteer in the third world
14. Go to antique auctions
15. Go camping (you may meet a guy at the campsite or the camping gear store)
16. Join a motorcycle club
17. Take some supplies to the local animal shelter
18. Attend a recital
19. Take part in the summer workshops that take place when colleges are empty
20. Get dressed up and drink cocktails at a swanky hotel
21. Sit by a fountain on a very hot day and enjoy an ice cream
22. Join the navy
23. While away your time at a sidewalk cafe
24. Organize a BBQ for your neighborhood

25. Join a local computer club
26. Try dog sledding in Lapland
27. Sit on a jury
28. Join a book club
29. Take flying lessons
30. Donate some blood
31. Try caving (spelunking) or pot holing
32. Go on safari in Africa
33. Try hang gliding
34. Send for tickets to your favorite TV shows
35. Go to a country show or rodeo
36. Take a trip to the zoo at weekends (lots of single fathers)
37. Have a night out with friends at a comedy club
38. Take a computer software training course
39. Go to yard or garage sales, car boot sales (UK) and flea markets and see if you can get more than a bargain
40. Join a debating society
41. Visit a transport, automobile or locomotive museum
42. Visit a ranch or farm
43. Arrange to meet a female friend in a hotel bar and get there too early
44. Go ice skating and see who you skate into
45. Visit a jazz club
46. Try kick boxing
47. Have a night out at the opera or classical music concert
48. Browse at a music store or stall that sells old records
49. Join a writers group
50. Try a whiskey tasting class
51. Find an extreme sports event and watch or take part
52. Talk to someone every time you have to stand in line for something (ATM, bus, morning coffee, concert tickets)
53. Buy a model airplane or R/C plane for a male relative from a model airplane hobby store and ask for advice. Or try flying one yourself in the park.
54. Try a pottery, woodwork or sculpture class
55. Join a treasure hunt/go metal detecting
56. Find out about nature walks in your area and join one

57. Set up a badminton net in the park and play with a friend (Have a couple of spare racquets available).
58. Go on a ghost tour at a local tourist spot
59. Go paintballing with a group of female friends and find some male "enemies" to shoot
60. Take fencing lessons
61. Visit a small town rodeo in Colorado, Idaho, Utah, Wyoming or Montana
62. Join a bungee jumping experience day
63. Go to a boxing or professional wrestling match
64. Start collecting coins/stamps/vintage comic books/old movie posters or similar and have fun talking to people who may have something you can add to your collection
65. Shoot a bucket of balls at the practice golf range
66. Ask a guy for directions on the street
67. Join a bird watching or beekeeping club
68. Play Dungeons & Dragons
69. Take part in an organized long distance walk
70. Train for a triathlon
71. Try an improv class or acting workshop
72. Sell cakes at work for charity so you have an excuse to go desk to desk (get permission first)
73. Attend a self improvement workshop
74. Visit a skate park. Just watch him show off if you don't want to take part
75. Eat at a sushi bar
76. Go to a random happy hour in your city once a week
77. Sign up for a bicycle tour
78. Kick a soccer ball about in the park with a female friend and guys can't resist joining in
79. Take a part-time job working for or as a caterer
80. Take a weekend trip to where guys go on bachelor (stag) parties
81. Get your house painted, the roof repaired, a new bathroom or a kitchen fitted and guys who make a good living from their practical skills will visit you!
82. Learn to shoot at a rifle range/gun club

83. Go to an investment seminar
84. Browse the equipment in a sporting goods store and ask for advice
85. Attend Chamber of Commerce events
86. Go to an athletic event (anything from college sports to the Olympics)
87. Play Frisbee in the park or on the beach and let him join in
88. Work part time in a bar or restaurant frequented by the kind of guys you like

And the point is? You can meet men anywhere, so get out and do something!

WHAT TO DO WHEN HE CATCHES YOUR EYE

It's only one part of the battle when you find someone you like the looks of. You have to actually engage with him in some way to make him notice you and get to know him. If you have been regularly chatting with people of all types just like we talked about earlier in the book, your task will be easier.

Out And About

If you're shy then I encourage you to practice, practice, practice engaging with people of all kinds as well as guys you like. That's the only way to get over your shyness. The way to make the uncomfortable comfortable is to make it a habit.

There's no doubt about it, you will get more dates and meet Mr. Right faster that way. And there's really nothing terribly difficult about making an off the cuff remark here and there. It's no skin off your nose if he doesn't take up the reins and chat.

He might be married, engaged, preoccupied or otherwise not interested. You lost nothing. You don't look stupid or like you're throwing yourself at him, if you're friendly to everyone. You're just one human engaging with another via a quick comment and a smile.

In many cases, it's the only way you'll ever make contact with a guy you like outside those places where men go to pick up women, or where it's natural to talk to anyone in a social setting such as a dinner party, volunteer group or work event. A guy is unlikely to approach you standing in line for coffee, or shopping for groceries, but by making a comment, he'll be happy to continue the conversation if he's interested because he knows you are friendly and approachable.

For help with making those opening comments, see Appendix B.

In A Bar Or Nightclub Type Situation

If you're out for the evening with your friends, you might be hoping guys approach you without having to make an effort. If you spot someone who catches your eye, you might look over in his direction to let him know you noticed him and hope he'll take it from there.

Although you looked at the guy, and you're thinking if he's interested he'll approach you, chances are he won't make a move whether he likes the looks of you or not. Most guys have stronger reasons for leaving you disappointed than they have for speaking to you. Here's why:

1. You Weren't As Clear As You Thought

Either he didn't notice your look or he imagined you were looking for someone (perhaps your boyfriend) or the bar. Most guys are poor at interpreting body language, so you have to make it really clear that you like him before he'll even think of making an approach.

2. Embarrassment And Fear Of Rejection

He's not sure if he has read the situation correctly, and if he's mistaken he'll be forced to go back to his friends with his tail between his legs. The more public his approach, the less likely he is to make it. It doesn't matter how attractive you are. In fact, the hotter you are, the more he thinks you'll reject him and therefore the chances of him approaching you are like snow in the Sahara.

3. He's Not Interested

He already has a girlfriend or a candidate in mind. He's married or gay or simply wants to spend time with his friends. Perhaps you're not his type.

What To Do

If you want to get to know a guy in this type of environment, you have to make sure he notices you noticing him, and work out if he's interested or not. This is the difference between those women who regularly meet guys when they are out on a Friday or Saturday evening and those who don't!

1. As soon as you notice him, look over and catch his eye, then turn back to whatever you were doing.
2. After a few seconds, while he's still wondering if he imagined it, look again for a second or two and this time give a slight smile (not a full on grin)
3. The more confident guys might approach you at that point. If he doesn't do that during the next ten minutes or so, reduce the physical distance between you and move closer to him on some pretext.
4. Once you get within speaking distance make a casual remark about the music, the venue, the crowd, anything to get the ball rolling.

Don't think that it's unfeminine to be the one who approaches. As long as you are casual about it and equally friendly to others in the room, not just the guy you singled out, there's no loss of face, if you don't get a response.

Do You Always Have to Be The One Who Starts A Conversation?

No, you don't necessarily need to start every conversation. By going out a lot and going to those places where there are a lot of men, you'll naturally come into contact with many potential dates. The more confident guys will approach you more readily than guys who are not so confident, but if you go regularly to the same place, Mr. Average Confidence may pluck up the courage to talk to you before you talk to him.

98

It just seems a pity to wait because:

- You can cut out a lot of wondering and hoping by just starting a conversation and finding out from an off the cuff remark or two whether he's interested. If he's not, you can move on without wasting time.
- While you're waiting for him to talk to you, some other girl with a bit more courage might be getting her hands on him after starting a conversation with him. Why risk it?
- By not practicing the opening gambit with as many guys as you can, you are never going to get better at it, and so you'll always be limited to those guys who approach you. It's much better to be the one choosing than to wait to be chosen. Honestly, a lot of guys go around in a world of their own not noticing potential dates and will never talk to you unless you open your mouth first.

Of course, if alpha male type super confidence is an essential for you in a guy, waiting for him to approach you is a way to sift those guys out! They will count themselves in by being the ones to talk to you. Just be careful because super confident guys are often players who are well-practiced in talking women into sex, but they're not looking for anything long term.

YOUR ACTION PLAN

Well done for getting this far in the book. At this point:

- You know who you are looking for and you also know to avoid automatically rejecting more than 99.9999 percent of the male population by having the perfect guy in mind who doesn't actually exist
- You've thought about the kind of things you might need to do to be ready for Mr. Right when he shows up
- You have lots of ideas about where the kind of guy that will make you happy hangs out
- You have some ideas about how you might signal interest when you see him

It's time to put everything together and create a concrete and personal plan to follow. This means deciding on the action steps you're actually going to do, not just reading about them in a book.

Step One

Make sure you're ready for dating; that is, you're in the right frame of mind, and you're looking and feeling your best. Make a list of anything you need to do. This is personal to you, of course, but may involve things like this example

- Book a therapy session to help finally let go of the ex
- Look for new hair styles and book an appointment at the salon
- Buy a book on boosting confidence and carry out the exercises
- Practice flirting with everyone. Aim to talk to three strangers (male/female/young/old) every day from now on

You can decide if you need to complete this plan before you start looking for Mr. Right. My advice is not to wait until you think you are completely ready. We are all a "work in progress" and will never be perfect or even the best that we can be. If you wait until you're ready, you might never be ready!

Step Two

If you haven't done the exercises to think about who Mr. Right might be, (see the Know Who You Want To Meet Section), then now is the time to get clear about this.

Step Three

Once you know the kind of guy you're looking for, think about all the places where he is most likely to show up from the ideas in the sections on places to meet guys.

Step Four

Pick out all the ideas for meeting Mr. Right that

- interest or appeal to you
- are accessible/affordable/available in your locality
- show you at your best/make you feel relaxed and happy

Create a concrete plan for showing up in these places (or taking part in that activity or whatever) for at least five of those choices.

If you are struggling to come up with five from all the ways there are, it probably means that the whole meeting Mr. Right exercise is slightly (or even a long way) outside your comfort zone.

The thing is, comfort/discomfort is a relative thing. How comfortable are you about being alone for the rest of your life? Spending Valentine's Day without a partner when everyone you know is paired off? Being the perpetually single female at family occasions? Often the best things in life are just outside a barrier you set up for yourself in your mind. So go on, be brave and pick the five that seem the least difficult to tackle.

Step Five

Make a commitment to taking action, not just a vague promise like, "Someday I'll try speed or online dating," or "I must try that new sports bar sometime."

Break your five choices down into small action steps and decide what order you'll do them in. Make sure you can do the first step of one or two of your choices this week. You don't have to do everything at once - most of us have full lives as it is - but you need the feeling that your plan is moving forward and taking shape, so you can keep the momentum going.

For example, if you've decided that you'd like to try rock climbing, as you've picked that out as a great way to meet sporty, active guys, but you've never tried rock climbing in the past, your plan might look something like this

- Search local venues/training courses on Google (when? Tomorrow)
- Find out if I need any special clothes/shoes/equipment (when? Tomorrow I may as well research this at the same time)
- Book a training course or a session with an instructor (when? Book something this week, choosing the first session I can make in the future)
- Decide if I'd like to make this a regular activity (when? After the initial course, not based on how many guys were at one venue but on whether I liked the activity!)
- If I like rock climbing, try all the local venues, clubs or meetups. Strike up conversations with at least 3 other climbers at each one. Ask for help where I need it.
- Think about a vacation or weekend involving a rock climbing element suitable for beginners as well as more advanced climbers.

Plans for some activities may be much simpler...

- Shop for food on Friday night when single guys are most likely out and about and speak to 1-3 guys who are on their own at the store
- Check whether the same guys shop regularly there at the same time every Friday
- Repeat the exercise with a few different stores

OR

Visit the local art gallery on Saturday on my own and comment on the art work to three people (guys if there are any there, but if not, whoever I find to get used to striking up conversations with everyone)

Step Six

Keep following the plan for each choice until you decide that you've pursued it for long enough.

Don't give up at the first hurdle. Always give everything a fair trial. If you're doing something new, it's never easy at the beginning. Keep going until it becomes more comfortable. But if you know in your heart of hearts it's not for you, then give up that activity or going to that venue.

If one of your choices doesn't work out, replace it with another. If you get through your initial five, add more options from the longer list of appealing activities/places.

Repeat until Mr. Right shows up (and you're sure he's Mr. Right).

Of course, there's no reason to drop most of the activities you take up, just because you found your guy. By this point you may be enjoying visiting galleries and museums, windsurfing, hiking or chess or whatever you've started doing. Continue to enjoy them!

A lot of the things that you have been doing to meet guys make you a more interesting woman to the guy you're with. If you chose the right activities (ones that you are truly interested in) your life will be richer and more fun for doing them, so why stop?

You can still be your best self, friendly and open. It's part of what keeps you irresistible to the one you're with, as well as attracting him in the first place.

TROUBLESHOOTING

If nothing seems to work, it's likely to be the result of one of the following three problems. There's no need to panic. They are easy to correct once you recognize where you are going wrong.

Problem 1: You're Flitting About

You may have your plan in place, but you're jumping on board with so many options that you never do justice to any of them.

If you decide to give hiking a go and turn up at a hike or two, and then the following week you decide that's not for you, drop it and turn your attention to swing dancing or scuba diving, you are not really giving yourself a chance to get to know anyone.

You may have worked out that there are no decent available guys in that hiking group after two weeks, fair enough, but you haven't given yourself a chance to enjoy hiking, to get to know your companions (or to get to meet their brothers, guy-pals, or co-workers, for that matter). Nor have you given yourself the opportunity to get interested enough in the activity to book a trip farther afield with better pickings (perhaps with one of your new friends).

105

If you're a social butterfly like that, just skimming the surface and never going deep with anything, you'll have trouble forming relationships.

There's nothing wrong with having a lot of interests or a lot of friends, but if none of your interests go any deeper than two visits and your new friendships are never getting a chance to get off the ground, you're not truly expanding your social circle, which is what you need to meet new guys.

Problem 2: You're Not Engaging With Anyone

If you go out a lot but you're keeping to yourself, you will not meet as many guys as you could, because there are not many guys who are confident enough to approach you without being given a very clear signal that you would welcome that.

In a social situation where you are involved in some kind of activity, it's easy for you to make contact by requesting assistance, talking about the activity, or asking a question. Even though a guy you have your eye on could talk to you just as easily, it still helps you get to know more guys if you are the one who kicks off the conversation. It makes him notice you and see you as a friendly person, open to talking to him.

On a night out, in a busy bar or similar venue, or in a queue at the coffee bar, it's more difficult to find a topic to start a conversation but not impossible. See the Love From Ana free guide (details in Appendix B) for help with that.

If you're not doing anything to engage at all, you will be left with only those guys who are super-confident about approaching girls. And these are generally the ones who hit on girls all the time. You are destined to meet mainly the players and pick-up-artists of the world.

Problem 3: You're Showing Signs Of Desperation

If you feel like you've tried everything in the book (including the two troubleshooting ideas above) and nothing has brought you any closer to meeting a special guy, it's time for a rethink.

Chances are that you have become too focused on getting a guy and have forgotten to focus on yourself. You have forgotten to have fun and enjoy yourself and become too needy. It's as if desperation is seeping through your pores and frightening off every eligible guy within 10 miles.

It's all to do with your mindset.

I'm all for taking action but if your every thought and deed is focused on getting a guy, your life is out of balance. The secret is in taking action, but being detached from the result.

This means making sure you look your best, going out a lot, being friendly and open, and organizing a ton of interesting things to do and then just letting things happen. You let life unfold as it will.

This feeling of detachment stops you from pushing away the very thing that you want. Your detachment or desperation shows in your face when you're not detached.

Detachment is another form of confidence. If you have it, you know your own worth and that good things will happen to you if you do the right things. You don't have to force the pace or get impatient. Confidence or detachment, whatever you call it, is one of the most attractive qualities you can have. And the opposite, desperation, is one of the most repellent.

If you're getting upset that the right guy isn't showing up, despite all the action you are taking, it's time to restore the balance.

Even though it may feel counter-intuitive, forget about men for a while and focus only on you.

This means not making yourself more attractive for the sake of a man, not going where men will be found, not thinking about men at all. But it also doesn't mean making yourself deliberately unattractive, avoiding places they frequent and never talking to them.

Just treat them as a natural part of life's tapestry. They are there. They'll always be there. It's time to think about what you want for you.

After all, you are the only person who can make you happy. A man does not arrive with happy pills.

If your days are dull and boring and you have no vision of how you want your life to be, then it may be that you have been relying on a man to rescue you from your routine existence. But no one should expect anyone to do that. You're not living in a fairy tale waiting for your prince to rescue you from a deep sleep.

In other words, don't be an extra in the movie of your own life. Be the director! As a single woman, you have the freedom to shape your life as you want it to be.

What have you always wanted to do but haven't dared to try? Do it!

Perhaps you need to think long and hard about what you would like to achieve. It doesn't matter if you don't already have your ultimate vision nailed down. Think about it and begin!

This is not a trick to dupe yourself into thinking you don't really want a man, so don't think you can just stumble along until "he" shows up.

This is for real. This is what you are going to do to be happy, supposing he NEVER shows up.

- It could involve changing careers.
- It could involve retraining.
- It could involve changing countries.
- It could involve a complete lifestyle change.

Who knows?

But whatever your "focus on you" plan is, if it's the right one, it will make you feel alive like nothing else. It has to be truly what you want. You, and no one else.

As a result you'll be happy with or without a man. But it's one of the ways that he'll show up for sure, and when you're least expecting him!

This is the equivalent of a woman who has been trying to conceive a child for years, and who suddenly becomes pregnant only when she stops stressing out about it, decides to adopt or resigns herself to not having a family.

It's a bit soon for baby talk when you haven't even found a guy yet, but you know what I mean.

Great men love independent women who have their own lives. They don't want the needy ones, the ones waiting for him to make their life complete. They want a woman who is already whole and knows her own worth, who has the type of life he would love to be part of – one that he almost has to beg to be part of.

When he shows up, don't make him beg, will you?

FINALLY

APPENDIX A: IS FINDING A MAN WORTH THE EFFORT?

All around the Internet you'll find articles about how hopeless boyfriends are. You know the kind of thing you find with a quick search

- 20 Reasons Why A Best Friend Is Better Than A Boyfriend
- 5 Reasons Why Having A Plant Is Better Than a Boyfriend
- Why Having a Knitted Boyfriend Is Better Than A Boyfriend
- 7 Reasons Why a Lover Is Better Than A Boyfriend
- Dog Or Boyfriend? Five Reasons Why Dogs Are Better

It's a disturbing theme, though fun to read if you are feeling a bit down about not having a man in your life!

But is it really worth going to a lot of effort to find a boyfriend, who may end up breaking your heart or causing you a lot of aggravation you don't need?

Most of us think it's worth the risk, because when things go well, there's nothing quite like falling in love and that feeling when he loves you just as much as you love him.

To balance all those "boyfriends are a waste of space" type articles and to help your motivation, if you're hesitating about doing what it takes to meet a great guy, here are some reasons why having a boyfriend, or at least the right boyfriend (not Mr. Wrong) is a great idea.

- You'll always have someone to do something with, even if it's just hanging out at the mall or relaxing on the sofa with a good movie.

111

- You'll have someone who loves you for yourself...foibles, flaws, idiosyncrasies and all. He'll even find them cute because they are part of you and that gives you confidence.
- You can be more open with him than you have ever been with anyone else because you know he loves you.
- You'll know someone who thinks you're beautiful even on a bad hair day.
- You'll have someone who respects you and considers you when he makes plans.
- You'll never be without a date on Valentine's Day, Thanksgiving or any other special occasion.
- It will stop your family constantly asking when you're going to get a boyfriend.
- You'll have a shoulder to cry on when things to go wrong at work, someone who supports you no matter what.
- You won't feel like a spare part when your friends who are in couples invite you to do things with them..
- You'll have someone to have fun with on vacation, and you'll be able to visit all the romantic places in the world and enjoy the romance of them with someone special.
- You can show your sexual side without fearing that he will think you are "easy"
- You will feel all warm inside when you think of him.
- Endless hugs and kisses
- A strong pair of arms for when you need a stronger pair of arms than you have
- You can make him feel manly by asking him to deal with spiders and other such things you'd rather not look in the face
- You can eventually marry him, have kids and grow old together, if that is what you want and he is in agreement with that plan!

APPENDIX B: FREE GUIDE

For a FREE guide on How To Start A Conversation With A Hot Guy so that you you don't stand there all tongue-tied not knowing what to say when a guy you'd love to go out with is standing right next to you in the coffee shop, airport check in or elevator, click here

http://lovefromana.com/talktohim/

You'll also get more essential tips and updates from the Love From Ana site for finding the love of your life and making him yours, and the chance to download other valuable free reports including

- How to Be Irresistible – Find A Man And Keep Him Forever
- Chocolate Body Paint Recipes And Ideas (Naughty but nice!)

Love From Ana is filled with practical advice for women who want something special in a relationship, whether it's someone you just met or a lifelong partner. If you want a loving, romantic, supportive, mind-blowing relationship with a guy in your life, take a closer look at the Love From Ana blog here.

http://lovefromana.com

CONTACT ANA

Feedback, questions and comments are welcome. You can get in touch via this email address:

ana@lovefromana.com.

Ana says:

"I'd love to know, above all, which of the 182 places you are going to explore and where YOUR Mr. Right was hiding in plain sight! Cure my curiosity and I'll be forever grateful."

If you liked this book and want to be part of the reader panel who review pre-release copies of future books, please send an email to ana@lovefromana.com mentioning you would like to to take part.

You're also welcome to join in the fun by commenting and sharing here:

Blog: http://lovefromana.com

Twitter: https://twitter.com/lvfromana

Facebook: https://www.facebook.com/lovefromana

Made in the USA
Monee, IL
20 December 2022

23037713R00068